Portraits of Magnolias

In the Shadow of Elvis

Portraits of Magnolias

In the Shadow of Elvis

Milly Hockingheimer

Copyright © 2011 by Milly Hockingheimer.

Library of Congress Control Number: 2011919652
ISBN: Hardcover   978-1-4653-8122-4
        Softcover   978-1-4653-8121-7
        Ebook   978-1-4653-8123-1

All rights reserved. No part of this book may be reproduced or transmitted in any form or by any means, electronic or mechanical, including photocopying, recording, or by any information storage and retrieval system, without permission in writing from the copyright owner.

This book was printed in the United States of America.

To order additional copies of this book, contact:
Xlibris Corporation
1-888-795-4274
www.Xlibris.com
Orders@Xlibris.com
107151

CONTENTS

Seeds 9

Sprouts 23

Blossoms 30

    Patsy Kay 38

    Becky 51

    Johnnie Kat 63

    Lena Sue 70

    Hally 74

    Betty Mae 95

    Claudia 107

    Letitia 123

With Love and Memories of
Juliet Archibald Hockingheimer
Aunt Millie, Aunt Edith, Jimmy, Duck, Betty, and
Robert E. Hall of Memphis

With Thanks and Love to
Theodore A. Gowdy—Teebo I (Tebo),
Robert, Sandra, Del, Lee, Bobby, Jack Lewis, Charleen, Sheila,
Ruth, Joanne E., Fentress,
Gerry and Charles, Bill, George, and
The Ferrells

Special love and thanks to Geralyn C. Phillips
for being the lone member of my Reading Committee—
a very difficult assignment especially with the time crunches—
and Teddy and Aunt Millie for listening all the way through—twice!

A special thought of Puppy Ham Wuppy

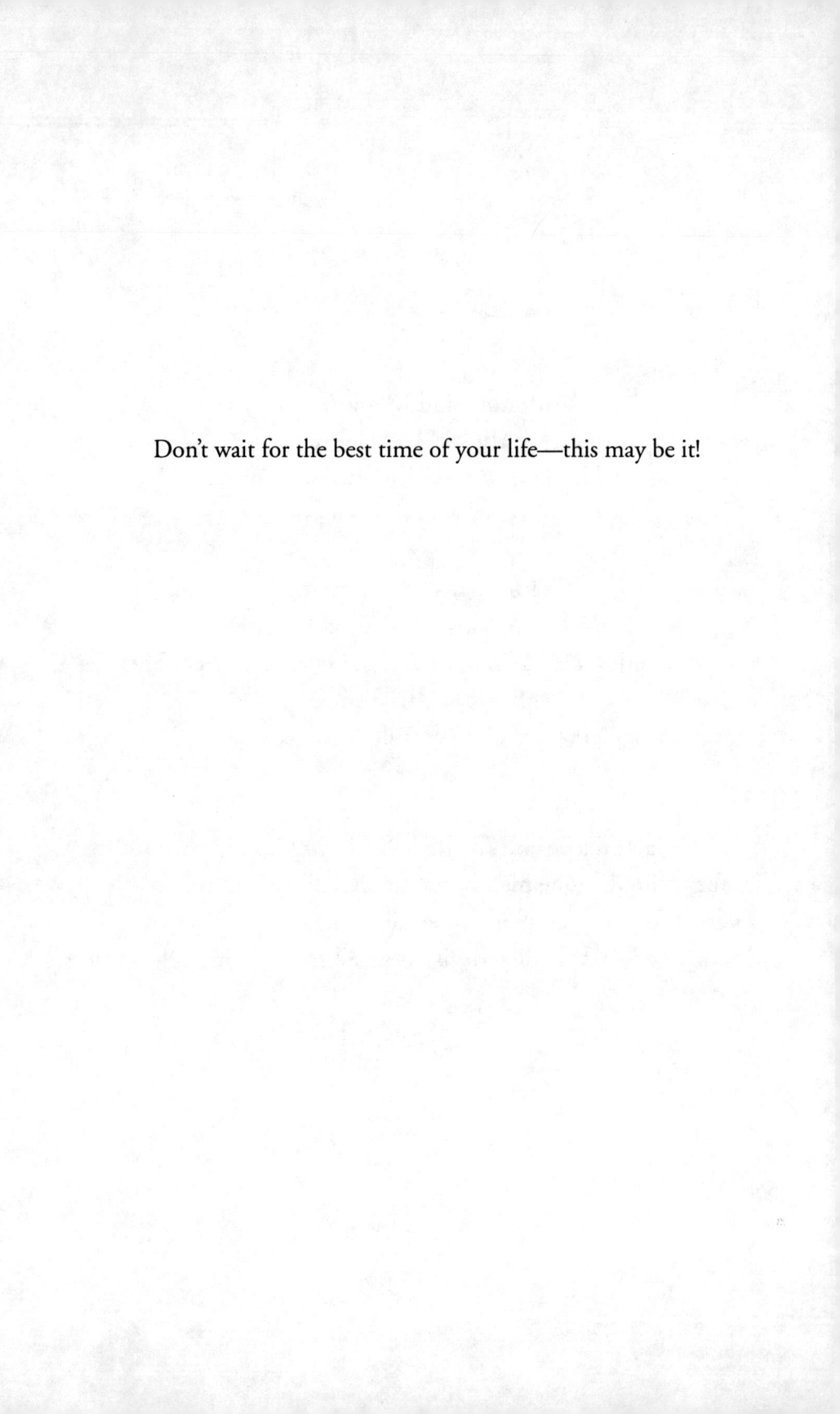

Don't wait for the best time of your life—this may be it!

Seeds

I WOKE UP to see that the world outside my second-story window was entirely white. Everything. The ground. The roofs on the houses. The cars. The trees.

"Mama!" I screamed with great alarm. "What's all that *salt* doing all over the ground?!!?"

My first memory—this pristine white blanket below me—was one of the few snowfalls that ever covered the small town of Addison, which offered a safe, sheltered life, very little of which took place outside its city limits. Although a few years before some of its young men had returned from their first travel abroad, it had been a pleasure trip by no means—but they *had* stopped Hitler. Until I was in high school, they were the only persons I knew who had been outside the United States of America.

My mother's parents died when she was very young, and Mother and Aunt Margie were raised by various aunts and uncles, of which there were plenty in Addison. My great-grandfather was with Robert E. Lee when he surrendered at Appomattox, after which Edward Roberson walked the long way from the state of Virginia to Addison and his young bride. Their children were born in Addison and Edward Junior's children were born in Addison—my mother and her sister, my Aunt Margie. During World War II, my mother was living with Aunt Margie and her family in another small town while awaiting my birth, and I was therefore born in the nearby state capital. But in a few weeks I was in Addison, too, so being born elsewhere didn't count—because although my name was Margie King, what *did* count was I was a *really* a Roberson.

The town had been named for a Civil War hero who was the conductor on the first train that had stopped there; Addison was small, and it seemed I was related to most people in it. Edward Junior's brother had six children—five boys—all of whom served their country during World War II—and a girl, all of whom still lived in Addison, none with less than three offspring. Most of them were named Roberson, but even if they were not, they were *known* as Robersons. As I was.

The ribbon which is time did not seem to unravel there on the edge of the Mississippi Delta. People who live off the land often mark existence by nature's events, and the original settlement had been right on the banks of the Tallahatchie River, where the cotton could be easily loaded onto barges for transport and an ample supply of catfish could be caught and fried for supper. Everything was just measured in terms of the acts of God—natural disasters, who died, and who had a baby—"That was the storm that hit right after ol' Miz Thrailkail died—must have been '32 or '33—must have been '33 since Lottie Jo Myers had her baby and Josh's in high school now." Life and death, the universal calendar.

The Old Benedict House, built before the Civil War, had been vacant for about twenty years. Although the Carsons bought and renovated it and spent more money on it than if they had built a new home, it was still The Old Benedict House. Charles Bernard's family bought it next, but what they sold a generation later was The Old Benedict House. No matter how many families would buy it, no matter how many times it would change hands, it would remain The Old Benedict House until time or progress tore it down.

Conversation sprang forth about sickness and illicit endeavors, and if you could not be the first to report an errant husband carrying on with a divorcée, you had better know who had just checked in to the local hospital. And then the race was on to see who would be the first to deliver soup to the family home of the patient, if not the deceased.

Social life revolved around the church, represented by several denominations. The various ladies' circles met on Monday afternoons, and for those ladies who worked during the day, other circles were held on Thursday nights. After choir practice on Wednesday nights there was prayer meeting for all but the Presbyterians, who were of course otherwise predestined. Sundays church went on all day—Sunday school, "church" (the 11:00 a.m. service), youth fellowship, evening services, and social hour; the Baptists (so numerous that there were two distinct factions) had B.T.U. in between—so the bouncing, chirping youth of Baptist Training Union could descend upon the hungover Saturday-night incarcerates at the jail and pound religion into their already-throbbing heads. Very few people were ever in jail. The citizens of Addison felt free to leave the doors to their homes unlocked, and when one could not find a parking place on the town square, it was customary to double park, leaving the key in the car in case it needed to be moved. Children rode their bikes all over town after dark.

My mother and Aunt Margie went to the girls' college in the state and then taught school until they had children. My mother was a very accomplished musician, and she always sang in the church choir, which she usually directed. She had majored in literature and was known to speak well on many subjects. To her mind education was right up there with air, food, and shelter. She was widowed shortly after I was born.

One Sunday my other aunt (on the other side of the family) from Memphis came to see us and took me back with her to visit for a week. I had a wonderful time at the zoo seeing the elephant and riding the merry-go-round. She even took me to Goldsmith's, the finest department store in the city, to see the models who swirled around our table while we dined. I felt very grown-up.

Her son Bobby was 12 years older than I but he never seemed to notice. He was extraordinarily kind to me, and even took me along when he went out with his girlfriend JoAnn. He had a contagious happy, sunny personality and went around the house singing. He played the accordion and would sit and serenade me. He was unusually talented, and he liked to take pictures. Our grandfather, who lived close by, would take Bobby to the gym where he taught him how to box. After Bobby was state Golden Gloves champion for two years, he became the most prominent photographer in the city, "Robert E. Hall of Memphis." I thought that was the most sophisticated phrase I had ever heard—and it probably was. One day he made a helicopter for me out of match sticks and glue. Before long he learned to fly and one day he flew down to Addison in a rented plane and landed in Mrs. Tuttle's cow pasture. The cows were unimpressed, but everybody else in town was and talked about it for weeks. This love of flight finally overcame him and he hired a photographer, turned the business over to my aunt, and became a professional pilot. He eventually flew all over the world, even over the Bay of Pigs for the CIA. He finally returned to Memphis to build a film studio, commute to Hollywood to direct tv shows, and since he could erase years from ageing stars with his expert lighting, he became the darling of them all.

Our grandfather was my only living grandparent. His was my first experience with death—but aside from having his last pictures made by Robert E. Hall of Memphis, no one in my presence made a big deal over it, so I did not see his demise as tragic although I knew I would never see him again. I'm sure this affected my attitude toward the death of my loved ones for my lifetime, that the deceased has gone on to something better.

After visits with my aunt, even though I was very young, I was put on the train, the then-glamorous City of New Orleans, by myself. There was no reason to fear that I would not reach home safely, as I was placed in the care of Howard, a porter known all along the Illinois Central line. The City of New Orleans had stewardesses, all of whom were trained as medical nurses, who were also responsible for me, but they were never the same. Howard was always there. When I would go to see Aunt Margie, I would be placed on the train by my mother, and Howard would see to it that I was delivered into the loving arms of Aunt Margie, who was always at the depot to meet me with my Uncle William and my cousins, Edward and Clyde. Edward, Clyde, and I would play Monopoly, Uncle Wiggly, Scrabble, and all the other games they had, and Superman. Edward would be Luthor, from whom Clyde as Superman would save me, Lois Lane. Aunt Margie kept every kind of ice cream imaginable in the freezer for her family and the crowd of their friends who felt free to drop in anytime, and we would interrupt our saving of the world—or Lois Lane's rescue—long enough to cool off during the hot summer days with mountains of ice cream or Eskimo pies. There was always an ample supply of Coca Cola because that's what Edward always had for breakfast. During the winters I was frequently sick with asthma and cokes made me feel better. They also helped my headaches, and they were always served at parties. I associated cokes with feeling good and being happy, and the refrigerator at Aunt Margie's house never ran out and I could drink all I wanted.

During one visit Aunt Margie took me to see "Heaven Knows, Mr. Allison"—I adored Robert Mitchum from that day forward. Edward and Clyde would also take me to movies and swimming at the country club. When they got older they even took me along when they broke in to the tennis courts after hours. One night we got caught and I was sure we were going to jail. The man who caught us was a friend of Uncle William, so after scaring us within an inch of the state penitentiary, he told us to go home and probably laughed all the way to his.

Clyde was named for my great-Uncle Clyde, who with his sisters Ozy and Phoebe, lived on the very edge of Addison in the last house before the woods. Uncle Clyde and I used to sit on their huge front porch and rock in the great white rocking chairs. It was there that he taught me to sing "Home on the Range." I didn't know what an antilo was, but I *did* know it played some kind of musical instrument while a deer played another.

By the house were a large garden, a barn, and a pasture beyond in which the cow grazed. Sometimes when I was very small I would spend the night, and in the winter we would sit in front of the fireplaces which furnished the only heat and roast marshmellows on sticks of kindling wood. Since we had space heaters at my house, I thought this was like living in the Old West. John Wayne probably did this same thing every night.

In the summertime, the woods blazed with lightning bugs, and many of them came into the yard, where Johnnie Kat Botty, who lived at the other end of the street, and I caught them and placed them in a jars with holes. I would lie in the darkness and watch the bits of light climb up and down the grass in the jar, and the next morning I would release the bugs to fly back to light the forest.

Before long the upstairs apartment gave way to a larger one across town. In the spring the huge yard burst with bright flowering shrubs—dogwood, crepe myrtle, and forsythia (a word never used—they were "yellow bells") among them. There were jonquils everywhere. Hydrangeas were prolific, blooming like huge summer snowballs in a rainbow of colors, perhaps making up for the absence of white ones in winter. Our landlady was known as "Battle" because of her blazing temper, which erupted from a body appropriately topped with flaming red hair.

One time she and her husband sued a real estate agent. In court Battle's husband said something on the stand that made her mad and she jumped up and hollered, "He's lying! Throw the son of a bitch in jail!"

The judge called for order, pointing out she had just called her own husband, her partner in life as well as the lawsuit, a liar.

"I don't care!" she screamed, "he's *lying*!"

Battle was very nice to me, however, and one day surprised me with a wonderful Raggedy Ann that she had made. It was my very favorite doll. Battle appeared every morning for coffee with my mother and began her recitation of events in town since her visit the day before. She knew everything and spoke freely in my presence; as a four-year-old child, I knew which married man was seen with what other woman, who had been drunk the night before, and who got what in any will.

My mother had opened a little shop in the back yard from which she sold gifts and baby items. The summers in Addison were hot, and the only air conditioned commercial establishment in town was the picture show. In the summertime between customers my mother would sit under the crabapple tree and shell peas. I had gotten a little pink chick for Easter that she called Velma. When Velma lost her pink color, grew a comb, and started to crow, my mother refused to call him anything else. Velma was very tame and, like everyone else, adored my mother. He would perch on Mother's chair, then her shoulder, and ultimately sit on her head. Mother never moved, and I don't know how many customers appeared in the back yard to find her with a lap full of peas and a rooster on her head. It never occurred to me that this might be unusual.

Burton Grafton was then the high school football star and after he graduated got a football scholarship to the University before being the first local son to make the pros. He often cut across our lawn as a shortcut home. He would come upon my mother sitting there shelling peas with Velma on her head and politely greet her, sometimes stopping to talk, as his mother and my mother had been childhood friends. Then he would go on home, having never mentioned the rooster or betrayed in any way that he'd noticed it. He did not seem to think my mother's sitting under a crabapple tree shelling peas with a rooster on her head was unusual either.

He and his mother lived in his grandmother's house, which was shaded by the largest, most prolific magnolia tree in town. The gentle scent of magnolias would float on the soft summer breezes, calling attention to the glorious white blossoms nestled in Miss Melvina's tree. She would sit on her porch sipping iced tea, and about once a summer when she would see me passing by, Miss Melvina would call to me and get a contraption—sort of a broom handle with a large clipper on the end—out of her shed. She would take this tool, which was taller than she was, and clip a huge magnolia for me. This was thrilling to me because the magnolias grew so high in their trees that I rarely got to see one up close. She would give me a really big one which would have filled my small arms, but I was very careful to hold the stem and try not to touch the huge white petals so they would not turn brown. My mother was as delighted as I at these wonderful gifts and would find a wide, deep dish or rather flat bowl for it and for most of the night I would watch the magnificent white flower, with its red cone in the middle. They had turned brown by the time I woke up the next morning, but this was a special event for me one or two nights a year. I thought God probably placed these beautiful flowers so high up so they couldn't be easily picked and more people could enjoy them longer.

When I was five years old I was compelled to go to kindergarten, as it was standard procedure to be taught at this time by Miss Maude Harmon, who had taught all of the local parents centuries before when they were in elementary school. Kindergarten started much too early in the morning and I hated it passionately—except for recess when we would run to the edge of the yard and wave to the engineer in the passing train, smoke trailing behind, as he blew the whistle at us and waved back to us as he sped on down the line to Aunt Margie's and faraway places. In kindergarten I became part of the group of girls that until high school graduation would be bound together by blood kin and the small choice of playmates available in a town of Addison's size—Claudia Seaton, Patsy Kay Humphrey, Hally Jordan, Sarah Jane Mosely, Betty Mae Cochran, Letitia Sullivan, Lena Sue Crawford, Johnnie Kat Botty, Sallybeth Waltrip, and Becky Smith.

I was spared some of this kindergarten attendance because of a case of measles, and Letitia and her little sister Bonnie, who lived on Carrollton Avenue in the house with the steeple (shaded by the Grafton magnolia tree across the street), brought me a bouquet of pansies, which I loved. They had a playhouse in their back yard—not a draped card table, but an actual, small house in which our little bodies could actually stand. The pansies grew on each side. The next week the pansies were still fresh when I took some of them to my cousin Terry, three days younger than I, who was taking his own turn with measles and relishing his absence from Miss Maude's. I was very impressed that his mother kept his room totally dark.

Terry was Junior Roberson's son, which made Terry "The Third," the first The Third that I had ever known. Each Christmas morning every branch on the Roberson family tree would gather at Terry's grandmother's for a glorious morning of singing carols, thousands and thousands of presents, and a breakfast that could compete with the Harvest Supper held each fall at the Presbyterian Church, of which we were all members (except for Jake's wife, the only Catholic in town until they had children). There were so many children and adults there that they spilled into every room of the huge house. The occasion was totally joyous. To me, that *was* Christmas.

I wanted President Truman, who was constantly shown in the newsreels strolling all over Washington, to be re-elected. I don't know why, because my mother wanted Dewey. She was almost as devout about her Republican beliefs as she was about being a Presbyterian—even though everyone running for anything had to run as a Democrat in the one-party state. The rural communities nestled in the cotton fields would have rallies, and the politicians would stand on dusty stages in the hot summer sun to tell everyone why they (all men) should be elected. When there were state-wide elections, candidates would come into Addison and speak to everyone from the pavilion in the center of the square. Everyone. The merchants left their shops, the customers all poured out—the whole population on the square was interested, so little Johnny Grant would hustle over with his red wagon laden with his ice chest and jars of lemonade to quench the thirst of the town of Addison as the candidate droned on. Little Johnny made a killing by election night! One time the town doctor introduced a candidate for Governor, as they had been roommates in college. The doctor had to work night and day making house calls and all, so it was thought he must really like the candidate if he would take the time to introduce him. Someone locally personally *knew* one of the candidates! When the candidate got elected, this was our closest brush with political power until John David Farrell, the local attorney, ran for Governor and *everyone in Addison* then actually knew the state's chief executive! On election day in Addison, voters would amble over to the courthouse and mark their paper ballots with pencils. That night a group of town men (no women) would sit around at the courthouse and tally the votes. Bub Craig, my friend David Ross's father and an elder in our church, would let me sit at his feet under the table and listen. Bub was always the one who said, "Tally." I never said a word. The counting would start when the stores closed at six o'clock and go far into the night. During this process someone would run back and forth to the town square pavilion to keep the citizens (all of whom were present and either drinking little Johnny Grant's lemonade or eating his Eskimo Pies) updated until all the votes were counted. From my spot under the table in the Chancery Clerk's office, I knew the count before it was ever announced.

Princess Elizabeth in England was not elected, but she *was* crowned Elizabeth II. My friends and I stopped playing Movie Star for a few weeks to play Queen. That same year Eisenhower was sworn in as President. The evil Stalin died and could no longer order the atomic bomb dropped on us. I did not think Ike would have let anyone bomb us with anything anyway—he had led the crusade in Europe that saved the world for freedom, and I felt very safe living in his country.

When I was about five years old I met my first movie star when Lash LaRue, King of the Bullwhip, came to town. I marched right up to him in a department store, introduced myself, and engaged him in conversation. I later wrote to him requesting an autographed picture of him with his horse Rush, and it arrived shortly thereafter. He used green ink.

The next year I went to Memphis to see Roy Rogers in person. When I got to my aunt's house, I learned the he was to be photographed by Robert

E. Hall of Memphis! Bobby went to Roy Rogers' hotel and came back much later to report that he had met Dale Evans and that Lash LaRue had dropped by. The King of the Bullwhip was photographed with the King of the Cowboys and the Queen of the West by Robert E. Hall of Memphis! Bobby gave me a copy of all of the pictures that I wanted.

Every child in Addison would spend Saturday afternoon seeing westerns at the picture show. This began when one was about six years old and continued throughout elementary school. Terry and I would sit together, and first we would see a chapter of Captain Video, Tiger Woman, Superman or another serial, then previews, a cartoon, and finally a shoot 'em up with Gene Autry, Roy Rogers, Rocky Lane, Hopalong Cassidy or the Durango Kid. Terry liked Johnny Mack Brown, but of course my favorite was my very close, personal friend Lash LaRue. We would sit on the edge of our folded-up seats on the back row for the one o'clock show and see the whole smorgasbord again at 3:00 p.m. From the time he was about seven years old Terry had had a job swatting flies at Roberson Brothers grocery store, earning a penny a fly, but on Saturdays he did his swatting in the morning and was available by one o'clock. We never missed going to the show on Saturday. Despite the fact we saw cowboys routinely shot in the back, not one of my friends nor I grew up to be an axe murderer.

During the week I saw Alan Ladd ("Shane"), Burt Lancaster ("The Crimson Pirate"), Rock Hudson, Elizabeth Taylor, James Stewart ("It's a Wonderful Life" is the first movie I remember)—about whom I read in movie magazines to which I subscribed. In this way I could be more authoritative when we played Movie Star—until I met Lash LaRue, my boyfriend was usually Alan Ladd. Lash LaRue really got around. He had picked children out of the audience to be in his show (with his mighty bullwhip he lit a cigarette that he had a teenager hold in her hand), and as I progressed through adulthood, I found many friends and acquaintances had also actually met Lash LaRue, as he made many personal appearances across the South, particularly at State Fairs. To a person, they all commented what a nice person he was. I was not at all surprised.

I believe my mother started reading to me the minute I was born, and one of my favorite books was "Children of Other Lands" which had on its cover an Arab sheik riding his great black steed across the desert. I remember Nat "King" Cole's soft, velvet voice on the radio (few people in town had televisions), but Jo Stafford's lilting descriptions of the pyramids along the Nile, the marketplace in old Algiers, and sunrise on a tropic isle made splendid visions of exotic places reel through my mind. I could see myself in a large silver plane that took on a golden aura as the sun drenched its wings, and I could look down and see everything she described. My very first word had been "airplane" and flying always seemed to be a most wonderful thing. Soaring over everything on earth! At least one person in Addison besides the war veterans would go abroad—I would leave Addison and fly to see the sheik riding across the desert. And I *had* to go to Rome.

My mother's store had been moved to the town square by the time I was six or seven, and when I suffered with asthma she would call me between customers to read The Hardy Boys. She sold the books in the store and I read all that she did not read to me. My favorite was *The Secret Warning*. I never liked anything heartwarming, especially Lassie. I listened intently on the radio to Inspector Heartstone of the Death Squad; Mr. Keen, Tracer of Lost Persons; The Shadow; and Mr. Chameleon. The creaking door on "Inner Sanctum" scared me to death. Like the rest of America, I listened to Jack Benny on Sunday nights.

I spent a lot of time in my mother's shop. And as young as I was, I was frequently left in charge while she went to the bank or post office. I would wait on customers, sell something, take the money, and carefully wrap the gifts as Aunt Margie had taught me in her family's jewelry store.

My mother's shop was right across the street from the town fire alarm which was on the outside wall of the pool hall—probably placed there because the pool hall was always open. I never remember seeing it closed. It was not unusual for mother's shop to get the emergency call. It was therefore not unusual for me, minding the shop all alone, to go flying across the street into the pool hall to get someone to sound the alarm, since it was way beyond my reach. No woman in Addison had ever seen the inside of the pool hall, but I could describe it in detail. I never failed to startle a pool player who usually threw some crucial shot. I would burst through the door and in my high-pitched, young voice, scream for someone to sound the alarm! There was not a moment to lose! Hurry up! Hurry up! All eyes would fall on me, this tiny alien from the world outside invading the smoke-filled masculine domain. The manager was a huge man who of course knew my mother and that I was no doubt minding the shop. He would come to the front of the pool hall, squat way down to ask me where the fire was and go to blow the siren. As soon as I heard the loud wail begin, I would go back across the street and await my mother's return. Reporting a fire was serious business, not only because of the fire and danger it posed to life and property, but because it brought the entire town to a complete stop. We had no official, professional fire department and the alarm would summon men from their jobs for miles around who were volunteer firemen—no matter how important another matter might be, the fire took precedence over everything else. Others would come running to see if there were some other way to help—perhaps take the injured to the doctor's office. No one ever questioned that I was reporting an authentic emergency. When the town bought the new bright red fire truck, it was paraded with pride throughout the town and was frequently parked unattended in front of the fire house for all to see.

I also went to the bank and the post office on store business, and on the way back sometimes I would stop at the drug store with a friend and get a banana split from the then high school football hero, Von Graham. We would ask him to put it in two dishes—one with the pineapple, the other with the nuts. He'd just smile and make two banana splits, one covered with nuts, the other with cascading pineapple. I was very proud when my good friend made first string on the conference football team.

During the work week the stores around the square were usually open by eight or nine o'clock in the morning and closed at 6:00 p.m., except on Saturdays when the stores stayed open until nine o'clock at night. That was to accommodate the country folks—mostly cotton farmers who had that one day to come the long way in to town to acquire the few items they could not produce at home. I was astonished when I grew up and moved away and learned that the rest of the world worked 9 to 5 during a five-day work week.

Next door to my mother's shop was a camera store, which was usually attended by a young lady sixteen years old who had graduated from high school very early. She was not old enough to enter nursing school, so in the meantime she earned money toward her education. Betty Lou lived in a tiny rural community about five miles away and her mother brought her to work every morning. She became sort of a big sister to me and frequently took me home to spend the night at her family's big rambling house where she lived with her mother, her grandparents, her three brothers, and one sister. I would take my Baby Brownie camera to record the wondrous adventures I knew I would have. Her grandmother made fabulous banana pudding and whenever she knew I was coming, she would make two huge pans of it. I loved going there to spend the night. Being in such an enormous family to me was absolutely wonderful. On cold winter nights after supper and ample banana pudding, Betty Lou would herd her brothers and Jamie Ann and me into the large front bedroom, close the door, turn off the light, and tell us horrifying ghost stories. She would do the wailing, whistling, and screaming—or whatever it took—that would later on keep us awake all night waiting for the boogey man to come to get us.

Her brother Jay was only a year older than I and when I was there in the summertime, he would take me fishing in the pond near their house. We would have a picnic lunch, and afterward he would find some sassafras by the pond and make toothbrushes for us. I was sure this is what cowboys did in the Old West. It was on one of these fishing expeditions that I caught my first fish which was about six inches long. I wanted to keep it, so Jay found an old empty bean can and filled it with lake water and put the fish in it. The fish was dead the next morning, but by then the whole family had seen it.

I could not believe Jay could remember so many jokes and riddles, and he was so quick witted that he could keep everyone around him laughing, no matter what came up.

When I was in the fourth grade I was told Jay had rheumatic fever and had been brought to the Addison doctor's office to stay in bed to protect his heart. I went to the drug store and bought him some magazines and candy and went to the doctor's office to visit him. After several weeks Jay went home, but we did not know how much damage had been done to his heart. He still had to stay in bed and missed that year in school.

The kids of Addison looked forward to Halloween. We would dress up as horribly as possible (I had a hideous witch costume) and go around trick or treating. We could go alone or in small groups all over town. No one thought anything of it. Nothing would happen to us, and even if we were going to trick, the worst we would do was cake a window with soap.

About eight o'clock the adults went to a party at the home of Frank Throckmorton. Mr. Throckmorton *loved* Halloween even more than the children of Addison did, and his party had become an annual event. We children would go over to his house to trick or treat early in the evening before all the candy got picked over. His yard was made to look like a graveyard and had tombstones everywhere. Mr. Throckmorton had some of them rigged with gadgets that produced moaning from the ground around them, and dry ice was strategically placed so that the yard was engulfed in mist. He hung spun glass and ghosts in the trees, so the whole place looked very spooky. We looked forward to our Halloween excursions up Mr. Throckmorton's jack-o-lantern-lined sidewalk.

We were always invited in and were constantly amazed at the decorations—there would be witches and goblins flying from the ceilings of every visible room. On the dining room table would be orange punch and cupcakes and petit fours with pumpkins and ghosts drawn with the frosting. One year the home was fixed up like a haunted house. Another year the front rooms were Frankenstein's laboratory. After this initial foray, we would canvass the rest of the town for treats and return after the party was in full swing. Mr. Throckmorton went to a lot of trouble and planned his next Halloween party from the minute one was over. One Christmas Eve Mr. Throckmorton had to go to the doctor because he was concentrating so hard on making his fangs that he punctured his lip and had to have three stitches.

A day or two before Halloween Mr. Throckmorton drove around town in a hearse. If he were driving down the street and saw children waiting to cross at an intersection, he would make sounds come from the hearse like moaning or screaming. Sometimes he would get out his bullhorn and yell, "Help me! They're going to bury me alive!" The children would holler and scream and flee from the scene—only to find as many other kids as possible to meet Mr. Throckmorton at another intersection to get the daylights scared out of them again. Someone said Mr. Throckmorton had an arrangement with an undertaker in Memphis to use a hearse because Mr. Dinkins at the local funeral home took a dim view of Mr. Throckmorton's Halloween activities and certainly would never have loaned him his.

There was one thing that was standard procedure at all of Mr. Throckmorton's Halloween parties—Mr. Throckmorton made his entrance by having a coffin wheeled in from the kitchen by ghouls. The coffin would be placed in front of the fireplace in the dimly-lit living room while dramatic organ music played, and then Mr. Throckmorton would slowly rise from the dead as Dracula. He would climb out of the coffin and very ceremoniously swoop around his guests swirling his cape and saying, "Goood evvvv-en-ning!" as he appeared to be eyeing everyone's throat as a tasty morsel. He insisted on answering the doorbell himself after his rise from the coffin in order that he might scare to death any late little trick-or-treaters. We all knew Dracula would answer the door, but we screamed and carried on anyway, and Dracula/Mr. Throckmorton never would let on that he knew we had visited earlier and would give us more huge portions of candy and usually some of the punch in paper cups and again show us around and point out the latest additions to his Halloween decorations.

In junior high Claudia and I were researching James Tillotson Addison for history class and went to the funeral home one day to see if they had any information we might find useful. We went in the front door and there in the vestibule was a dish containing tiny calendars with a happy face on top. The back of the calendars could be peeled away, to reveal a sticky surface so that the calendar could be stuck on a wall. Just under the happy face was the inscription "Happiness is Sticking with Dinkins Funeral Home."

We filled our purses with the calendars and went on down the hall to the office. We passed the casket room, and Claudia wanted to go in to have a look-see. Mrs. Throckmorton was seated at the little desk where the sales person sat. We greeted her and as we stood next to the desk we saw a sketch of the cemetery and two X's in a square labeled "Throckmorton Family Plot." Apparently the Throckmorton's were planning their funerals, so we did not want to intrude and started perusing the caskets. We saw Frank Throckmorton talking to Mr. Dinkins on the other side of the room. I could hear Mr. Throckmorton saying, "But I don't *need* to buy one for *myself.* I *already have* a coffin at *home*. It fits me perfectly, and it's so *comfortable*!"

Mr. Throckmorton sold life insurance.

Sprouts

I TOOK DANCING lessons when I was in the first grade. So did Hally Jordan and Betty Mae Cochran, whose mother taught them. This ended for me in the third grade when Johnnie Kat Botty and I began taking art lessons. Betty Mae kept up with the dancing lessons, and when we were in high school, she began teaching them herself. My art lasted for three years until I began taking piano lessons.

Traditions die hard in the South, and just as every generation had to be schooled by Miss Maude, children who took piano had to take their lessons from Miss Effie Perkins. Long after she could no longer hear her telephone or the doorbell ring, she still had as many students as she could get into her schedule. If a child were ill and could not come to take a lesson, the mother had to go to Miss Effie's home and beat on the window and wave wildly until she got Miss Effie's attention—or that of the little student then serving his/her thirty-minute sentence at the keyboard. No one seemed to question how Miss Effie could teach music even though she couldn't hear a thing and frequently went to sleep during the lessons. My mother didn't think Miss Effie could ever play worth a toot, so she arranged that I buck tradition and take lessons in a neighboring town. I was quite relieved, as Miss Effie had blue hair.

Little did we know that a lot of music tradition was about to be shattered. Unbeknownst to us, an obscure, youthful truck driver in Memphis had recently paid $4.00 to record a song for his mother. I was about to embark on piano lessons, but the truck driver was about to transform the music of our lives.

Mother drove to my music lessons in Junior Roberson's car, as his daughter, my cousin Sandy, also took these lessons. I adored Sandy, who was a year older than I and my role model. She knew how to do everything and she did everything well. Once she found out when my birthday was and gave me a surprise party. I was thrilled that she thought this much of me. It was she who taught me how to ride a bicycle, and she always taught me the latest dance steps.

Over the years we took piano lessons there were plenty of new steps to learn—like the bop and the stroll and the twist—the young man from Memphis, the former truck driver, was beginning to be heard on its local airwaves—which reached Addison, and he was changing our music. The swing of the teenagers of the '40's and the jitterbug had come to an end—the teenagers of the '50's would *rock'n'roll*!

When we went to Memphis, we would get a Top 40 list, and more and more often the new singer would have songs at the top. Patsy Kay took it upon herself to do some research about him, even going to Memphis to be on "Dance Party" with Wink Martindale. I tell you, Patsy Kay could be very thorough—the young man had gone to Humes High School, and one day he had gone into a recording studio ("on Union Avenue" quoth Patsy Kay) and made a record for his mama's birthday present. The secretary liked it and told her boss, ("Sam Phillips") who got him to make a record which got played on Dewey Phillips' ("no relation") local radio show one night ("July 8, 1954"). WHBQ's switchboard lit up. Dewey had to play the record over and over, first one side and then the other.

From that night on, there was a new sound in Dixie. The singer became interwoven into the fabric of our lives. He did not dress like anybody else, but before long the boys around school were dressing the way he did. His hair was not coiffed with the crew cut or flat top—his long hair was combed up and back in a pompadour and he had long sideburns. As he became better known, the boys started letting their hair grow. He had a strange name we had never heard—Elvis. Our parents got nervous about his ducktail haircut—which started being imitated by the local boys as soon as tall, lanky Teebo Vincent got his blond sideburns perfected with the swoop just so over his ear—but mainly about Elvis' gyrations while he sang. And *he* was not using a hula hoop. RCA bought the Presley contract from Sam Phillips at Sun Records, so we figured Elvis would be singing more since he must be on his way to New York. Elvis soon bought a green ranch-style house for his mother (who Patsy Kay said was named Gladys) in a nice section of Memphis, at 1034 Audubon Drive. We understood Elvis paid $500 down. It became quite the thing to drive by the house and jump out of the car to snatch a blade of grass for a souvenir. Some of the more adventurous fans would sneak with a vial all the way up to the house, as the ultimate status symbol became a few drops of water from Elvis' pool, I guess in lieu of Lourdes. On Sundays the cars drove bumper-to-bumper past his property. I went to visit my aunt, who, although knowing we would be stuck in traffic all afternoon, nevertheless placed her car in line just so I, too, could see the house. The whole family went—"to take Margie." We heard that Elvis could not go out in public without drawing a crowd, so at night he would rent a whole movie theatre, a whole skating rink, or even the entire Memphis Fairgrounds where there were a lot of carnival rides, so he and his friends could have some fun without being mobbed. Right before Christmas, Goldsmith's Department Store would open in the middle of the night just so Elvis could do his Christmas shopping.

Preachers all over the country warned parents that Elvis would make juvenile delinquents out of their darling children and send them down the happy road to hell. But public demand got so frenzied and intense, in 1956 Elvis was making appearances on national television shows such as Steve Allen and Ed Sullivan. When Sullivan said what a nice young man Elvis was, calling him a "decent, fine boy," parents calmed down, rationalizing that Elvis was only a flash in the pan and would soon be forgotten. I guessed a weekly sage such as Ed Sullivan carried more weight than the Elvis-condemning evangelists—as evidenced by the fact that everyone watching Ed Sullivan was missing the Sunday night church service anyway. Besides, despite the Top 40 lists, pilgrimages to Memphis in the hope of getting a glimpse of The King, and the growing stacks of Elvis records, about the only den of iniquity we teenagers in Addison could muster up was the corner behind the high school auditorium where some other boys joined Teebo Vincent to sneak a smoke at recess. We couldn't understand why the evangelists couldn't see that if the youth of America were at chaperoned parties dancing to Elvis records, they could not very well be out robbing banks at the same time. Had they not noticed that everyone who met Elvis talked about his respect for his elders and his good manners? Why, he yes ma'amed and yessirred people to death, and "Thank you very much" had taken on unanticipated national significance.

Every morning in seventh grade homeroom our teacher would go row by row, asking for any news anyone wanted to report. Although the intent was to make us aware of current events of world or at least town importance, someone (usually Patsy Kay) would invariably give the Elvis Report—where he was, his latest record, famous visitors to his home.

Eisenhower was still President of the United States and had engineered an armistice in Korea. In 1956 he thanked Dr. Jonas Salk on behalf of all 164 million Americans for developing the vaccine for polio, the horrible disease we feared. Grace Kelly had become a princess when she married Prince Rainier of Monaco (the Prince was also a The Third) and everyone learned how to pronounce it. John Wayne was making another generation feel safe, too. In 1958 he gave Joanne Woodward her Academy Award, and when Edward R. Murrow visited them on "Person to Person" her husband Paul Newman said he could make salad and popcorn better than anybody else. Over 99% of the 7 million cars sold in the United States had been made here. Walt Disney had opened the Magic Kingdom, and when I saw him welcome Art Linkletter and his many children to its opening, I knew I had to go there. Some day I would. Rome, the burning sands of the desert—and *Disneyland*.

I had acquired a number of interests by this time. I still ran around taking pictures and had graduated from my Baby Brownie to a Brownie Hawkeye, and various mothers were teaching us how to play bridge. Bridge was considered necessary to social survival for any female in Addison. No one in town could beat me at Canasta.

"This Week," the magazine section of the Sunday paper, ran three articles on extrasensory perception. I was fascinated. When Hally or Claudia would come over to visit, one of us would try to conjure up the thought of the other. I started reading all I could find on precognition, clairvoyance, and telepathy. Dr. Rhine at Duke University was studying ESP in a lab. One Sunday night I was studying in the wee hours of the morning. My mother came into my bedroom and sleepily told me she thought I ought to go to bed. She then turned around and went out, closing the door behind her. I thought she might be dead and had just paid me a good-bye visit. I was afraid this would be confirmed if I went to check on her. Maybe if I didn't go to find it were true then she'd be alive tomorrow. I worried about it the rest of the night. The next morning when I went in the kitchen, I was greatly relieved to see her standing there. When she found out how upset I had been, she was shocked. She never again told me to go to bed or came into my room late at night.

About this time someone found the remains of an antebellum mansion out in the country off an obscure branch of the Dam Road, so called because it led to the reservoir which held in check the Tallahatchie River. The ruin had been covered with foliage for decades and forgotten. Sandy and I finally convinced my mother we should go home from our music lessons that way, and we sped from the piano out toward Beau Rivage

Castle, the name given it when it was decided that it was haunted. But we were going in broad daylight and since we were predestined Presbyterians, we were certain we had nothing to fear. As we surveyed the huge space once occupied by Beau Rivage, I envisioned the grand balls which must have been given there before the Civil War, with the belles whirling around the dance floor in hoop-skirted gowns and fanning themselves provocatively in the presence of young Southern gentlemen before they went off to the Civil War.

One of the dashing Confederate heroes who might have attended grand balls all over the area was probably James Tillotson Addison. It was he for whom the town had been named, and the house he built, occupied by some of his direct descendants, still stood high on the cliff overlooking the entrance to Rolling Hills. He was tall, dark, and handsome, and whenever anyone wanted anything done, they went to him. He was the local can-do entrepreneur. A major farmer in the area, he was responsible for getting the train to stop in Addison, and it was then that the main settlement moved from the Tallahatchie riverbank to the railroad, on which the cotton went straight up to Memphis to be sold shortly thereafter. He was the conductor on the train—part of the deal to get the train to stop. The railroad management knew of his reputation and that he could indeed keep order on the train or anywhere else. He was the fastest draw and surest shot in the state. He was also a very devout minister, and used his expertise as a marksman only when necessary. He distinguished himself during the War, and with all his decorations—mostly for valor—when he came home, he was a certified—but very modest—hero. This just embellished his legend. Stories about him abounded, from his brave triumphant stands against Yankees and criminals (not necessarily viewed as two separate factions) to the time he made the train stop along the line and wait an hour while he hired a carriage, went out to a cemetery to perform funeral services for the six-year-old daughter of a close friend, and drove back and hollered, "All aboard" as the train pulled out and went on its way. Not one word of complaint was ever issued to the railroad home office by anyone on the train. If James T. Addison had delayed the train, then it must have been "for good reason."

Most of what was known about Beau Rivage was legend—no one really knew its story. It must have been built specifically for grand entertaining, and though the footprint seemed to indicate all of the other rooms were 22 feet square, one which must have been the ballroom was 44 feet square and the doors to it were all wide enough that the ladies could sweep in without gathering up their hoops. Only part of the stripped plantation home was left standing after the Civil War and the land had passed on down through the family until Deke McQuaid started raising his family there. The grandeur gone, the fancy "Beau Rivage" gave way to "the McQuaid place." Part of the building left standing was repaired and petitioned off from the rest. Deke had three boys and made his living farming on the surrounding acreage. The whole family worked very hard in the fields, from sunup to sundown, and took care of the animals and the garden around the house. The story went that one of their teenaged sons, Donald, had developed an interest in the supernatural after finding some arrowheads around a part of the farm that was said to be a small Chickasaw burial ground. Donald began to research their legends and rituals, and as one thing led to another, he got interested in the various herbs they used for medicine and in their ceremonies. After a while, he started studying voodoo. Deke was very much opposed to his son's pursuit of this knowledge and whenever he found Donald studying or practicing a voodoo spell, he went into a rage. He forbade his son to continue what Deke considered blasphemy, but Donald kept trying in secret to study the occult beliefs practiced generations before him. He had to be very careful that his father never noticed any of his books missing from their shelves. In the barn one afternoon Deke caught Donald reading a book on voodoo. Deke grabbed the boy by his overalls and slung him so hard across the floor that the boy landed sprawling, hitting his head on the opposite wall. Deke stormed out of the barn, sorry he had flung Donald so hard, but terribly troubled that his son was delving into the mysterious ways of voodoo. He was sure his son was flirting with danger and was determined that he would stop.

The next day was Saturday and Donald decided to go fishing. He had not seen his father all morning and thought that was just as well. It was a bright, sunny day, and he figured the Tallahatchie would be bursting with catfish. He also knew his father would be very pleased to have a big mess of cat for supper. He kissed his mother on her cheek and set off down the path through the woods with his dog Fella. His mother could hear him whistling as they disappeared from sight. She began to worry when Donald was not back home for supper, and even Deke was concerned when his son did not appear after dark. He took a lantern and went out to look for him at Donald's favorite fishing spots but could not find him. He stayed out all night, but not finding his son by morning, he marched, still in his work clothes, into the middle of a rural church service to ask for help. Brother Scott blessed the searchers who had immediately volunteered, and they spread out in all directions to look for the missing boy. Neither Donald nor his dog was ever found. Deke was inconsolable and blamed himself for the loss of his son. Deke stopped working the land, it became overgrown with foliage, the family abandoned the house, and since it was so far out in the country, it was seldom called to mind and eventually forgotten until some hunters had found the ruin about the second year Sandy and I took piano. After our on-site inspection, Sandy and I enjoyed our new status as the most up-to-date authorities on Beau Rivage.

Exploring abandoned houses out in the country was a frequent activity for the kids around Addison. Some of the old houses still had furniture and other artifacts in them. And it was much more exciting if the property were explored in the dead of night and were supposed to be haunted.

One glorious sunny Sunday afternoon in the spring, Sarah Jane Mosely, who did not have a driver's license but did have her daddy's new Chrysler for the afternoon, went around gathering the other thirteen-year-old girls that had been a group since Miss Maude Harmon's kindergarten class. By the time Sarah Jane had picked up everyone, there were twelve teenaged girls in the car. From that day we were known as "The Twelve."

The Twelve drew names at Christmas. The Twelve gathered at the summer coke parties given by Sallybeth Waltrip when Shelby Dell Clark, her friend from way over in the delta, came to visit. The Twelve would spend hot summer days together out at the dam, sunning, swimming, picnicking, and gossiping about everybody who wasn't there. The Twelve had pallet parties and invited no one else. Anyone who had been sick or out of town—or for any other reason dictated by a cruel fate had not gotten in that car that day—was left out of things until long after high school graduation. I knew full well that even though my mother was a Roberson, a family with tradition and generations of rock-solid citizens of Addison and sons of the Civil War and World War II behind it, had I not been in *that* car *that* day, a social stigma not of my own making would have been mine. I didn't even like all of The Twelve. I didn't know of any of The Twelve who did. But that didn't matter—what mattered was we were all ***friends***.

* * *

Blossoms

CLAUDIA BALFOUR SEATON was one of us squished in Sarah Jane's car that auspicious afternoon and was the second of three daughters born to Mr. and Mrs. James Balfour Seaton. No one *ever* called Mrs. Seaton "Claudette."

James Balfour Seaton rightly took great pride in the fabulous meals he whipped up when he came home each day from overseeing the town as mayor and several civic organizations. Mrs. Seaton never cooked anything. His spaghetti was to be died over and his catfish (which he caught himself at the reservoir) and hush puppies, accompanied as it always was by french fries, cole slaw, iced tea, and fresh strawberry shortcake, was legendary. From earliest childhood (after I met Claudia in kindergarten) I could not wait to spend Friday nights at the Seaton home. Mr. Seaton always welcomed Claudia's friends and kept encouraging us to have second helpings, even of the desserts. He always made enough so that we would find an ample supply when we later raided the refrigerator.

Mine was the only mother of The Twelve who had not forbidden her daughter to smoke; I was, therefore, the only one who didn't. Not much was known back then about the dangers of smoking; what *was* known was that nice girls did not do it.

Claudia smoked more than anyone else in school. She learned how one night while we were in the seventh grade when Hally Jordan had a pallet party at the small country club in order that we could "have a serious discussion" regarding Elvis versus Pat Boone. We all crowded into the ladies room and Claudia, Johnnie Kat, Becky, Hally, and Patsy Kay went to work on the Picayunes (which Johnnie Kat stole specifically for this purpose from a carton in her daddy's desk) after Emily, Hally's mama, allegedly went to sleep. We opened the window so the smoke could be hurriedly fanned out in case Emily, who was sleeping in the area of the concession booth on the other side, approached. We would take turns coming out to breathe and keeping watch, never realizing all the smoke came right back into the building via the window Emily had opened by her bedroll. We heard her coughing all night and just thought she had a cold. The Christmas of our freshman year I gave Claudia a rhinestone cigarette holder which she kept at my house, the only place she felt safe to use it. Mrs. Seaton would have scalped her alive if she had ever caught her middle daughter smoking. Which is why I learned to drive when we were in the eighth grade.

Claudia drove to school in her daddy's pickup and, despite valiant efforts, had not mastered the art of driving and smoking at the same time. At lunch hours during school we would jump in the truck, speed to Shug's Drive-In to get hot dogs, and I would wolf mine down while Claudia headed the pickup toward the Dam Road. By the time we got there, I was finished dining, we would swap places, and while Claudia ate her hot dog I would drive until we reached the mansion of Bubba and Della Humphrey. I would turn in and loop their circular drive—I had not learned how to back up yet—and point us back toward the campus while Claudia lit up. By the time we reached the high school, Claudia had finished having her smoke and we were ready for old Miss Lola Greenway's history class, where we learned to recite the Presidents in order just as my mother and Aunt Margie had when Miss Lola was much younger. I was certain, however, that my mother and her sister (who thought at that time that old Miss Lola was indeed ancient) had not been clouding up the cab of a pickup truck with smoke beforehand.

That was the year Travis Dexter came to Addison to live with his cousin Jimmie Gayle Trambeau. Travis was from Seattle, for heaven's sake. None of us in the eighth grade had ever met anyone from that far away. He had a dark brown, shiny flattop with ducktails and dark, dark brown eyes—and about the whitest teeth I had ever seen. He did not have a daddy, and he had gotten into some sort of trouble with the law, but instead of going to a jail or wherever they put bad kids in Seattle, his mama had whined and wailed until the judge finally agreed justice—and apparently the state of Washington—would best be served if Travis were just removed from the state and given a strong male personality to look up to. She shipped Travis down to live with her sister Charlene, Jimmie Gayle's mama, so Jimmie Gayle's daddy could handle him. Charles Trambeau owned a bunch of stuff, to include the GM dealership, so Jimmie Gayle always had a new car to drive to Shug's. I don't think I heard Charles Trambeau *ever* say *anything*—even though he was a deacon in our church. We thought it was terribly exciting to have a juvenile delinquent in our midst! But we couldn't find out what awful deed Travis had done to be shipped so far south.

We immediately accepted Travis into our circle just because he was Jimmie Gayle's cousin and obviously Jimmie Gayle liked him. Travis and Jimmie Gayle were inseparable. They went to school together, were on the football team and lettered together, double dated (Jimmie Gayle had started going steady with Sallybeth as soon as he got his football jacket), and drove around a lot in one of Jimmie Gayle's daddy's cars. After the day they both walked into Sunday School wearing blue suede shoes, that became the mark of whether they were *really* dressed up or not. After Carl Perkins had made his hit record, "Go, Cat, go!" had become part of our language, and everybody thought when Jimmie Gayle and Travis wore their blue suede shoes, they were about as cool as anybody could get! Pretty soon Elvis recorded "Blue Suede Shoes"—he had known Perkins at Sun Records, and out of consideration for him Elvis refused to record the song that Carl had written on a paper bag until Carl had sold his own million.

From the time he was getting the cars, Jimmie Gayle always picked me up when he saw me walking somewhere. Now that Travis was usually in the car, I got to know him, and he was always as cordial to me as Jimmie Gayle. Travis early on said that he wanted to be called "Dex." We all thought that was a very spiffy nickname, and why not—our token juvenile delinquent was trying to start a new life. If he wanted a new name as part of his rebirth, we'd go along.

Jimmie Gayle was supposed to have some sort of good influence on Dex—at least that was the theory. We all thought that was kind of funny—not that Jimmie Gayle was bad, but if the guys around town were going to get into any mischief, Jimmie Gayle was always right there in the middle of them, probably leading the way.

Word was when Enid Whitley, the despised English teacher, got her whole yard rolled with toilet paper on Halloween, that Jimmie Gayle was the one who had climbed up in each tree and created no less than a work of art—sort of a white May-pole, tenting effect with colored streamers hanging down which were made from pink rolls. (Apparently Jimmie Gayle et al could not find orange and black toilet paper in keeping with the holiday.) Those trees had been growing there since before the Civil War and Jimmie Gayle got the toilet paper right up to the top of each. Why, it must have taken him all night—and he couldn't *possibly* have gotten started until after the football game! The next day was Saturday, and we students passed by all day to admire the sight, some even clandestinely taking pictures for posterity, as this was a standard by which future acts of mischief would be judged. Little Johnny Grant set up his hot chocolate stand on the corner.

As soon as she woke up and saw her festive yard, the indignant teacher had called Sheriff Brimley to report and carry on about the dastardly deed done to her. He immediately launched one of his famous big-deal investigations. Everyone at Shug's sat there and hee-hawed about the whole thing. Miss Whitley spent all day calling every lady in town to wail about the injustice of it all and get what expressions of sympathy she could extract.

The next morning the entire display had vanished. There was not a shred of toilet paper anywhere. It was as though Miss Whitley had made up the whole thing. But the next Christmas any old widow who couldn't get the star right on the top of her Christmas tree was promptly referred to Jimmie Gayle by any teenager in town. Jimmie Gayle would go over with his ducktail all freshly combed, slicked, and sculptured and yes ma'am them to kingdom come. After the star was safely in place, he would even stay for fruitcake and carry on about it until he departed, promising to give Charles and Charlene regards and tell them what a fine young man he was. Miss Whitley had told him to tell them the very same thing when he had complied with her request to top *her* tree. She never knew that he had only two months before topped every tree she had!

* * *

The Year 1957 was very important.

The Mid-South Fair was an annual autumn event in Memphis, and thousands of people came from the tri-state area and beyond. Our school closed one day a year just so everyone could go. This began one year when so few kids showed up during Fair week that it wasn't worth holding classes. This year our mothers allowed Hally and me to board the Continental Trailways bus and go to Memphis by ourselves to the Fair. They knew Billy Hooper, the band captain and main source of *Mad* Magazines on band trips, and Charles William Redwing, second chair trombone, would be on the bus, and I guess they figured Billy at least could call an ambulance. Hally and I felt very grown up, since we were the first of The Twelve to be able to go to Memphis on our own. I was bucking tradition again—no mama chaperones, only Hally Jordan, Billy Hooper, and Charles William Redwing. When that bus pulled out of Addison, Hally looked at me and said, "Well, we're in high cotton now!"

I did not realize it at the time, but this single event was a major step in my life. There was no porter named Howard on the bus. Howard would never be there for me again. But from that day I was never prevented from going anywhere for lack of an adult presence. Independence was mine.

In October the Russians shocked us all by getting into space first with Sputnik, but President Eisenhower reassured us that our space program was still on schedule. He sent 185 military advisors to a place in southeast Asia called Viet Nam.

The year was also important for Elvis. In order to have some privacy, Elvis searched for a more remote place in which to live. Word was he attempted to buy Mrs. Mangrum's farm off the Dam Road, but she was a staunch member of the Enlightened Morning Star Baptist Church and refused to sell it to him. Shortly thereafter, Elvis purchased a mansion known as "Graceland" out on a stretch of highway between Memphis and Addison called "Bellevue Boulevard." But Elvis either hadn't heard of Patsy Kay or he had underestimated her. We had to pass Graceland and the pink Cadillac parked there every time we went to Memphis, and despite its high walls and guarded gates, Patsy Kay soon made several announcements to the effect that the person sitting in the candy-striped jeep at the entrance to the estate was Elvis' uncle, who was now her very close, personal friend with whom she had regular visits. When we passed Graceland and saw a whole fleet of Cadillacs and other cars parked one behind the other up at the mansion, we spread the word that Elvis was back in town. Elvis was well known for buying cars, sometimes for people he didn't even know. We could not *imagine* anyone could have so much money. He was *really* in high cotton!

Elvis proceeded to redecorate Graceland. One time on a trip back from Memphis, passing Graceland, Sallybeth got her mama to pull over so she could see what was going on. She learned that Elvis was having an entire room covered in carpeting—the floor, the walls—even the ceiling. It turned out to be the famous Jungle Room. Somehow she came away with a swatch.

Elvis was very generous with his money when it came to Memphis, its charitable causes, and its underprivileged. He paid hospital bills for persons who couldn't pay them—picked up the tab for surgeries performed on people he had never met. He would even show up unexpectedly at Baptist Hospital to visit a stranger he had heard was seriously ill. He never publicized any of this, but stories like this were in the Memphis *Commercial Appeal* all the time. Eventually Bellevue Boulevard was re-named, "Elvis Presley Boulevard." But apparently a church didn't care how fine and decent Ed Sullivan said Elvis was or how much he did for the underprivileged in their midst. We heard that the church made such a fuss that the portion in front of it had to be re-re-named "Bellevue Boulevard"—only to have "Elvis Presley Boulevard" resume at the end of the block.

Elvis did a great deal for Memphis besides give it more prominence on the map. He made its tourist business boom. When he started making movies in Hollywood, people all over the country stampeded to Memphis to see the home of The King. In 1956 the top two movies had been "Giant" and Elvis' very first film, "Love Me Tender." Entrenched as we were in the very home state of the President of the Confederacy, we did, however, get a real kick out of the fact those Hollywood types had Elvis rockin'n'rollin' way back during the Civil War.

Although we were pleased about Elvis' success and his getting famous and all, we wondered what the commotion was all about—it was just Elvis who lived up the road a piece. We had heard his music and kept tabs on him for years. He had been a presence in our lives. It had not occurred to us that everyone else in the world had not been hearing him all that time or known who he was. The excitement at this new talent was totally lost on us—we had been excited over him for quite some time now, and the new had long since worn off. He was ours.

1957 was also the year I was elected to the Student Council. I was delighted to serve while Billy Toll, the captain of the football team, was the president. We all knew he would get a football scholarship just as Burton Grafton and Von Graham had done. For some reason we kept supplying great college football material. I heard people say it was because of Addison's pure artisan spring water.

That December I saw my second snowfall and my first white Christmas. The snow began falling about three days before. Everyone was thrilled and ran outside to make snowmen while they could, and Terry and Sandy and I scooped up the cold white crystals and their mother made my first snow ice cream. Little kids went nuts seeing their first snow. We expected all the snow to be gone in a day or two. But the snow kept coming down. It continued to come down until we had three feet of it all over everywhere. There was no snow-removal equipment, as this was the Deep South and snow was not something we normally experienced. The whole town was immobilized. The school was closed and few people even ventured out of their houses for fear of slipping on their steps, which had become steep, dangerous inclines of ice. There was no reason for the merchants to try, because they weren't going to have any customers anyway. The men who worked at service stations tried to get in to help with emergency gas and tire chains. People kept tabs on the old and infirm, and the sheriff's office called them every morning to make sure they were all right. None of our houses had been built for this kind of icy onslaught—they had been built to keep cool breezes circulating throughout in the steamy summer heat. Now cold drafts were blowing throughout and we were freezing in our homes. We huddled in them wearing layers of clothes and walking from room to room draped in afghans crocheted by various ancestors. Claudia said she had put an extension cord on her electric blanket so she could get around her house. Charles Trambeau had a big powerful jeep that could get around fairly well in a pinch, and he volunteered Jimmie Gayle and Dex to take groceries and medicine to anyone in need. They were on call to escort the town doctor to be certain he got to house calls and emergencies. After a day or two, neighbors could help each other out with food and other needs. Ladies in Addison spent a lot of time canning—vegetables from the gardens, fresh fruit, and it was nothing for several of them to pick up blue ribbons at the county fair for their preserves. So folks had plenty of food to share, and we could hold out several days and not get hungry. Just like their ancestors during the Civil War, the ladies of Addison rose to the occasion and were heroines doing their part. I imagined it was like living on the frontier—we just made do with what we had.

That year when school began, I was thrilled to see Jay had decided to come to school in Addison. So was the football coach. Jay was one of our best players, and the basketball coach was delighted when he went out for that team, too.

Elvis went into the army. Sallybeth and Hally wrote long letters to President Eisenhower imploring him not to let the army cut Elvis' hair. Elvis was offered a cushy job in the entertainment corps, but he insisted that he get no special treatment (probably why, Hally mused, that President Eisenhower allowed Elvis' hair to be cut) and served in a tank battalion. We never heard any of those Bible-thumping evangelists mention what a fine example this was for the youth of America. While he was still in training, his beloved mother, the Mistress of Graceland, died. Two months later Elvis was shipped to Germany. Millions of fans were, in the words of the King, "All Shook Up." The King was on foreign soil.

One Saturday Claudia and I were allowed to go to Memphis alone in order that she could see a dentist. After Hally and I had gotten back from the Mid-South Fair without getting murdered, things had loosened up for some of the other Twelve. We got on the bus and began to look for two seats together. Then we realized there were no women on the bus—the bus was *filled* with young men. Claudia and I looked at each other with trepidation as if to decide whether we would continue our trip, when one of the boys at the front, no doubt seeing our uneasiness, rose from his seat and said gently, "'Scuse me, ma'am—y'all can sit here together," and he moved across the aisle.

We thanked him and sat down with some relief near the driver, and the bus roared out on its way to Memphis. The young man explained, "We're all draftees on our way to Fort Chaffee, Arkansas. It takes 22 for a charter, and there's only 17 of us."

The guys seemed very happy—relieved, actually, to have us aboard, were very friendly and polite, and Claudia and I responded with conversation when addressed.

There was a radio playing in the back of the bus, and we heard Elvis' recording of "One Night with You." Then we heard a loud moan from the rear and one of the young men burst into tears. As he sobbed and wailed uncontrollably, Claudia and I looked back and asked if he were hurt or something.

"He's not injured, Ma'am," our new acquaintance volunteered. "He just got married last night and had to leave his bride early this mornin'. He just goes to *pieces* ever' time Elvis sings that song."

When Claudia and I announced that we would pass Graceland, the whole bus got excited that we would pass "Elvis' actual house." The guys had a thousand questions, and Claudia and I were hard put to remember all the details Patsy Kay had recited a million times. The young men, all somewhat nervous about what was awaiting them in the army, started relieving their anxiety by making Elvis jokes, talking about defending our country with him at their side. We alerted everyone just before we got to Graceland, and they all ran over to that side of the bus. I was surprised it didn't turn over. All the guys were utterly *thrilled* to pass the home of The King. We'd been passing Graceland on the highway for years, not giving it much thought, from long before Elvis was around. But now that Elvis had moved in, we realized that we needed to give it serious scrutiny.

* * *

Patsy Kay

THE VAST ACREAGE owned by Bubba and Della Humphrey out on the Dam Road was joined to more vast acreage owned by his brother Sonny. Total landholdings of the two siblings constituted a large part of the county. Sonny had a daughter by his first marriage, Jane Ann (mother of Sarah Jane Mosely), and his second wife Hortense had presented him with Patsy Kay and, finally, a son, Bubby Lee. This made Patsy Kay the aunt of both Jane Ann's children, though Patsy Kay and Sarah Jane, whose car had given birth to The Twelve, were in the same grade—and Sarah Jane was actually older than her aunt Patsy Kay. When we discovered in kindergarten that Sarah Jane was Patsy Kay's niece, we giggled and snorted about it all day long and called her "Aunt Patsy Kay" the rest of the week.

Patsy Kay was pudgy and when she was a sophomore in high school could still be caught sucking her thumb while twirling a lock of hair at the back of her head. She envisioned herself the mother confessor to us all and felt it her obligation to tell all that she heard, as she deemed the height of her popularity directly corresponded to the volume of gossip broadcast. The only thing she felt lacking in her climb to "Most Popular Girl" was a boyfriend. This she would obtain at all costs. The only thing was, none of the boys ever asked her out. She would head out to Shug's and hang around for hours on end in the Buick that Sonny let her drive around town starting from the time she reached the age of fourteen. No amount of latest bulletins could get her invited to the picture show on Friday night.

But that was before the boys from Twiler, a rural community ten miles away, started coming to Shug's en masse and she met Biff Johnson. Biff drove the fastest Impala in the two counties (his and ours) and he made it perform at top speed whenever he got behind the wheel. He worked in a garage in Twiler and as soon as he got off at the end of the day, he got cleaned up and headed to Shug's. There at Shug's Biff Johnson met Patsy Kay Humphrey. As soon as Biff found out how much land Patsy Kay's daddy owned, he was more than happy to take her to the picture show and then out the Dam Road to the reservoir for the submarine races.

Sonny and Hortense were delighted that their little girl finally had somebody taking her out. But then Sonny called the sheriff and told him he wanted to know all about Biff Johnson. The sheriff was more than willing to oblige since he was running for re-election next year. When he came back with the news that Biff had quit school in the third grade and his sister had not one, but two, illegitimate children, the horrified Sonny and Hortense forbade Patsy Kay to see her knight in Chevy armor ever again. But Patsy Kay was not about to lose the only boyfriend she had ever had. No siree. And besides, being forbidden to see him only made him more exciting! She'd just get the car on the pretense of going to the picture show, drop a carload of girls off at the movie, meet Biff at Shug's, go to the reservoir for a couple of hours, and pick the girls up when the movie was over. Sonny and Hortense never knew diddly squat about it until one night when they stopped by Shug's for a coke after prayer meeting and there sat Biff and Patsy Kay two cars away.

All hell broke loose! Sonny yanked Patsy Kay out of the Impala and dragged her kicking and screaming into the Buick where Hortense sat wailing and wringing her hands, presumably a prelude to wringing Patsy Kay's neck. Sonny then dumped his massive frame behind the wheel and scratched off in a hail of gravel that would have done Biff Johnson proud.

Patsy Kay resolved then and there that if she couldn't have a boyfriend, then by God she'd at least have a husband.

Hortense was always at the Ladies Night Circle at the Enlightened Morning Star Baptist Church on Thursday nights. Sonny would be at his usual perch asleep in front of the television in his den. One Thursday morning after what was known as The Showdown at Shug's, Patsy Kay walked out to school with her weekend bag, having told her parents she was going to spend the night with Cassandra Scruggs to study for the next day's history test. Although Sonny and Hortense had grounded Patsy Kay for all eternity, they were willing to do anything to bring up her F in history so they consented, not suspecting a thing. They should have—first of all, Cassandra had a D in history; second, there was no history test; third, Patsy Kay had never spent the night with Cassandra in her life; and fourth—and most important—Cassandra was not one of The Twelve.

Neither parent thought anything about Patsy Kay's leaving for school in high heels and her mouton coat. When she got out of sight of the house, she doubled back behind it to plow through the vacant lot that served as a shortcut to the high school. There she reclaimed the rest of the luggage which she had hidden the night before and struggled with it to the dirt road Sonny had cleared away as a first step toward selling the land for a subdivision. There sat Biff in the Impala, and they were off to Georgia. What they had not counted on was there sat Bubby Lee in the bushes, having followed his sister out of the house, wondering why on earth she would leave at that ungodly hour—she took a certain pride in always being late for school. He had really enjoyed all the excitement at home that Patsy Kay's liaison with Biff had produced—he could not wait to get back and relate this latest intelligence to Sonny, who was still at home devouring his morning grits. Why, his daddy would have a *fit*!

My home room was on the front of the high school, so I was among those who saw and heard Sonny's pickup truck screech to a halt by the elementary school building. He labored to its door as fast as his fat legs would carry him and in a couple of minutes he emerged with Hortense waddling at top speed toward the high school. They crossed the campus toward the principal's office and a couple of minutes after that, the booming voice of Malcolm P. Clovis startled all of us, "Cassandra Scruggs. Come to the principal's office on the double." Cassandra was in another home room so Teebo Vincent, knowing we were counting on him, in a sudden coughing spasm excused himself to get a drink of water.

Teebo was famous for getting a drink of water in a crisis. The teachers probably thought he was a sickly young lad who kept walking pneumonia. This time he stood outside and coughed mightily, gagging for good measure, and after an appropriate pause of about seven minutes, gave another performance beyond the door. When he came back he even carried a paper cup—Teebo was a man who saw to detail. He then scurried to the pencil sharpener, so we all broke our pencil points and joined him.

Mrs. Rice—no fool and dying to know what was going on—having also seen the spectacle of Sonny and Hortense rolypolying to our building—ordered us to be seated.

"Teebo," she said imperially, "since you seem so eager to talk to everyone, we'll just give you the floor. You may share your comments with us all."

Startled, Teebo looked around helplessly—but knew Mrs. Rice, a respected, favorite teacher, wanted the scoop, too. Teebo coughed again, took a sip of water for good measure, and began his report.

"Cassandra's catching hell in the principal's office—not from Malcolm P. Clovis, but from Sonny. Cassandra was shaken to the core and spilled the beans that Patsy Kay and Biff are on their way to Georgia, 'cause Patsy Kay heard they could get married there without parental consent."

He had our rapt attention.

"Sonny immediately called the sheriff," Teebo continued, "and from what I could see, Sonny seemed to be satisfied the sheriff was going to get on it—said something about the highway patrol!"

As we sat in the home room listening to Teebo and speculating, once again the booming voice of Malcolm P. Clovis could be heard.

"Sallybeth Waltrip and Becky Smith, come to the Principal's Office on the double."

Now *that* was a bombshell—we were astounded! We knew for sure Sallybeth was not in on the plot. What could *possibly* be going on!

We looked to Teebo, who was somewhat hesitant to try the drink-of-water act again. He looked at Mrs. Rice.

"How do you feel, Teebo?" she asked with great concern.

Teebo looked flabbergasted. "Well, I still have a little tickle in my throat."

"Perhaps you need more water?" Mrs. Rice inquired sweetly.

Teebo grinned. "Yes ma'am, I sure do!" and bounced happily out the door. Mrs. Rice winked at the class. We all looked at each other in amazement.

Teebo came back lickety split with another paper cup. He coughed slightly and cleared this throat before he sat down and addressed the class, "It seems Patsy Kay went out to Biff's parents' house one night with Becky and Sallybeth in the car, so Mrs. Humphrey wants them to show her and Mr. Humphrey where they live. Malcolm P. is calling Mrs. Waltrip right now to get her permission for Sallybeth to leave school to go with them."

Teebo never failed in his mission.

Sheriff Brimley was indeed "on it," as he immediately began tasting the barbecue at the victory party Sonny would give him election night. "Thank you, Patsy Kay Humphrey," chuckled Sheriff Buford Brimley, "you have just guaranteed my campaign!" Talbert Dinkins, the deputy, said over lemon icebox pie at Brown's Cafe that the sheriff got on the phone and within hours the highway patrols in three states were on the lookout for "that lowdown, gall-dern Biff Johnson," who had transported Sonny's minor daughter—"darlin' li'l girl"—across state lines. "Why, he'll never get out of the state pen!"

Hearing about it, Hally mused, "I think that 'darling little girl' bit is a mite much!"

After Sallybeth and Cassandra sat trembling in the outer office of Malcolm P. Clovis, they were excused from classes to assist the Humphreys in their search for Patsy Kay. Mrs. Waltrip came to join the group, as she was not about to let Sallybeth go without her out into the moonshine still-infested boonies of Twiler with the hysterical Humphreys, and when they drove off, there were five heads in the car pointing towards Twiler. Since the Johnsons lived out in the country on the other side of the little settlement, it was a tricky undertaking to find the house—after all, they had built it so it could not be found—moonshiners are not socialites. The posse coughed and wheezed every time Sonny turned onto yet one more dirt road.

"Pig tracks!" he'd hiss every time he found himself on another byway. "That's all these roads are! *Pig tracks!*"

Sallybeth and Becky would start coughing fits again to muffle their laughter and the fuming Sonny would bang his foot down on the accelerator again.

After winding and turning through miles of twisting dust, the group finally found the Johnson house hidden in thick foliage in the next county. Sonny got out of the car and went banging on the door. A small woman in a fresh, plain housedress opened the door only a crack. It was Mrs. Johnson, Biff's mama, and upon learning who he was invited Sonny in. Sonny gave the John Wayne forward-ho sign, the car was emptied of its delegation, and Twiler's latest tourists descended upon meek little Mrs. Johnson. Mr. Johnson emerged from his nap in the bedroom—it had apparently been a late night at the still—and both he and his wife were surprised to hear the latest news of their son. They had not seen Biff for about a week, as he had by this time acquired an apartment in Twiler. They had never met Patsy Kay, having been absent when Patsy Kay et al had come to call, and had not been certain Biff was still seeing her.

Mrs. Johnson's small ramshackle house was spotlessly clean and she had offered the impromptu visitors lemonade. Sallybeth said they seemed like sweet, simple people, and that she thought both Mr. and Mrs. Johnson seemed pleased that Biff had decided to settle down.

So the search escalated and raged on. Sheriff Brimley kept assuring everyone he was still on it, that Biff Johnson would be apprehended within hours. What no one had figured into the equation was Biff's expertise at suping up his Impala and his uncanny gift for evading the law—a finely-honed skill, what with his running back and forth from the family still out in the woods around Twiler. When school was out that Friday afternoon, no one had any word on the goings-on in Georgia. At the football game that night everyone was much more interested in the score out on the highway than in the stadium. So far Biff was running on the wide open asphalt for a touchdown. Sonny and Hortense lived two blocks away from the game, so there was a regular stream of would-be messengers to and from the stadium. At halftime no one at the concession stand could dispense anything but cokes and hot dogs—no information.

Saturday night everyone was hanging around the fire station next to the pavilion in the middle of the town square (where little Johnny Grant, ever the precocious entrepreneur, made a fortune selling cokes) or at Shug's, and there were runners back and forth from the Humphrey yard. There was a vigil at the home of Sonny and Hortense, and the Enlightened Morning Star Baptist Church was having a special prayer meeting to pray for the deliverance of Patsy Kay from the evil clutches of Biff Johnson. Teebo Vincent, half serious, joked they should have been praying for Biff. The Twelve had a pallet party at Hally Jordan's big house within sight of the Humphrey home and awaited bulletins from the dependable Teebo, whose parents never cared what time he came in—he could stay out until daylight as long as he showed up at school during the week and at church on Sunday. Sheriff Brimley never pulled him over either, since Teebo's daddy was tax assessor and that would be unseemly and seen as a violation of professional courtesy. Teebo had taken advantage of this convenient situation earlier in the evening when he had made a run out the Dam Road to Tacawaw Henry's for a bottle of white lightning for the guys to drink outside the Humphrey's later on as they performed their sentry duty. Normally the guys would just sneak a few beers, but these were extraordinary circumstances calling for something more potent. Teebo was very generous with the white lightning, which all the guys appreciated, but actually Teebo told me one time that from the first swallow it burned all the way down. With his going through the ritual with Tacawaw and all, no one really noticed that Teebo really did not touch the stuff except for the ceremonial initial sip and then to pass the bottle around. It could very well be that evening that if the white lightning were from the Johnson family still, the guys might be helping to finance the very situation over which they were keeping vigil. Teebo was also ready to record any happenings for posterity with his trusty Brownie Hawkeye, something he considered standard equipment for any automobile he drove.

The procedure to get the white lightning "at the honk" was rather cumbersome, since Tacawaw, an old man with a scraggly beard and two bright gold teeth right in the front of his mouth, was a big fan of the high school band. He was utterly obsessed with it. He never missed a half-time or a parade. No matter how far away the football game was, early arrivals could see his beat-up pickup truck already parked by the portion of the stands closest to the section reserved for the band. Tacawaw never wanted to miss a note, pre-game or otherwise. He could not have cared less whether or not we ever won a football game. Before the season got too cold, he would put a folding chair in the back of the pickup and sit there with his ice chest full of RC's, eating his Moon Pies, listening to every note the band played. He would clap his hands to the fight song and stomp his feet to "Storm King" and "Band Festival." It got so our band director would give Tacawaw a friendly salute after the "Star-Spangled Banner" and a thumbs-up after the first march. That just thrilled ol' Tacawaw to death! Some of the parents objected to this little gesture of respect to Tacawaw, but they did not know that there was a secret between the band director and ol' Tacawaw in that when a child wanted to play in the band and there was no instrument for him and his family could not afford one, Tacawaw made an anonymous contribution to the cause. The child would be presented by the band director with the instrument of the child's choice at no cost. Tacawaw kept up with the children and when a band trip was coming up for which the child did not have funds, Tacawaw would visit the band director with an envelope containing enough cash to cover any needy children's expenses and an added dash of spending money. In some cases transportation issues might have prevented a child from joining the band—country children might not have a way home after late band practice or football games, especially the games out of town. The town taxi was always mysteriously available at these times. Everyone knew the driver and thought it was so nice of him to take the children home in the middle of the night, sometimes miles and miles out to their families' farms. No one but the band director knew how this gesture was subsidized—ol' Tacawaw saw to it all. I found out about this generosity one time when Teebo saw lights on late at the band hall and decided to investigate. He lurked outside a window open to the spring night and listened while Tacawaw delivered yet another envelope for State Contest. Tacawaw asked about specific children to assure they had what they needed—did So-and-So need new band shoes? It had been a while since Tacawaw had purchased the last pair and he knew the child had grown and might need a larger size. Teebo heard Tacawaw refer to his contributions as the Tacawaw Scholarship Fund and laugh with great gusto. Teebo and I pledged to keep this between us, since news such as this, despite the enormous contribution Tacawaw was making to the youth of the town, might be cut short by factions objecting to the source. Tacawaw obviously received great joy from his gifts and certainly the moonshine scholarships were changing lives.

Whenever the Teebo decided to make a run to Tacawaw's for the guys, he had to get Andy Brumfield, first chair trumpet, to go with him out to Tacawaw's juke joint somewhere way out past Nelson's Mills, near Oomishtwa Creek. Teebo would make a routine stop by the filling station to gas up and check his tires—"It's fifteen miles out as the crow flies and *this* crow dudn't wanna walk and push a flat tire."

Andy and Teebo would reach the outpost of civilization—I was never too clear about where it was exactly and thought that just as well—and saunter in, Teebo avoiding the rays of the single lightbulb hanging from a knotted cord over the pool table. They would try to look unobtrusive and like they belonged. This was usually unsuccessful, for not only were they obviously underage even if the whiskey had been legal, but there was Andy carrying his gleaming golden trumpet. The bartender, upon getting the hi sign from Teebo, would call Tacawaw from the crap game raging in the dive's back room, and Tacawaw would hurry into the front room, gleefully cackling and clapping his hands together, to welcome his young vistiors. He would unplug the jukebox, pull up a chair, push back the hat he had no doubt been wearing 24 hours a day for decades, cross his legs and arms, and with that golden grin, nod for the program to begin. Andy, in the light of the lone lightbulb, would brace himself dramatically with legs apart just like Ray Anthony or Harry James, take a deep heaving breath while raising the trumpet to his lips, and blow. He would play selections from "Bugler's Holiday" and "Trumpet Voluntary" in order for Teebo to be allowed the privilege of buying the hootch. The other patrons, none of whom had had this much exposure to culture in their lives, would stare dumbfounded and transfixed at the apparition before them, but when Andy was finished they would applaud delightedly, wondering what on earth these Martians were doing in Tacawaw Henry's. At the end of the concert, Tacawaw would nod to the bartender, Teebo would exchange the bills for the brown bag the bartender sneaked to him on the other side of the bar, and the guys would strut to the car, successful in their mission once again.

Sunday the church congregations from the Enlightened Morning Star Baptist Church to the Mount Israel Church of Christ prayed for the safe return of Patsy Kay Humphrey. (We understood the Feel Good Gospel Church of the Devine in Twiler was praying for Biff.) Monday the math lesson consisted of what had gone on over the weekend and studies in English II speculated on the future. This went on until Thursday night when Patsy Kay and Biff appeared at the Humphrey home as calmly as you please. They just got out of the Impala and slowly started walking up the sidewalk toward the huge white house.

Suddenly Hortense flew out of the front door, tears flowing, wailing, "Lawzy, Honey, Lawzy!" and she crushed the surprised Patsy Kay to her huge breasts.

"We're not married, Mama," Patsy Kay struggled to say. "We decided we're too young."

"Lawzy, Honey," Hortense replied, and thereupon gave the heartiest bearhug to the mystified Biff that he had ever gotten in his life, even from Jessie Maynard with both her legs wrapped around him.

"Come in, come in! Lawzy!" Hortense kept wailing, tears still streaming down her face as she tugged at the thunderstruck couple. "Darlin's, come in!" After the door shut, the vigilant sentries around the property heard nothing. Nothing. Either Sonny hadn't exploded or his gun had a silencer. No one came out for the rest of the night. Anyone who called the house got a busy signal. Even the ladies of the Enlightened Morning Star Baptist Church.

Patsy Kay didn't come to school the next day. Hortense hadn't appeared to teach her classes since she had gone to the principal's office. Our football team had an open date on Friday, so everyone was at the picture show when the famous couple appeared that night to make their grand entrance. And grand it was! Patsy Kay had on a white lace dress (the one she wore at eighth-grade graduation, I recalled) which she obviously thought very bridey. It was so tight by now with all the shakes she had consumed at Shug's that I just knew it would split when she sat down—but she was so busy receiving her public that the occasion never arose. She had on white gloves, carried a white sequined purse, and wore white satin pumps. Behind her the silent Biff stood around uncomfortably in his turtle neck and jeans. It occurred to me that in all the time I'd been in his presence—always at Shug's—I'd never heard him utter one word. I really felt sorry for him. A few people greeted him and shook his hand, but he just nodded politely and took a deep breath. He seemed relieved whenever he was ignored. I thought it would be a scream if he ever had to be in a room alone with the equally silent Charles Trambeau.

Mr. Randolph, the theatre owner, decreed free cokes and popcorn all around. No one really cared about the film which was being shown and as the projectionist was in the lobby along with everyone else to hear about the trip, the feature began an hour and a half late.

Patsy Kay took great delight in being the center of attention, a role never before awarded her. Although she was not up on the screen, she basked in the spotlight out there in the lobby as she related how she and Biff had gone all the way to Georgia and back, riding on the wind, untouched and unseen by the highway patrols looking for them in Mississippi, Tennessee, and Georgia. They should have looked in Florida.

Patsy Kay, gathering an air of wisdom about her, said, "We got to Georgia and decided we were too young to get married and then we decided to come back home."

Claudia leaned over and whispered, "She just got cold feet when she realized that they'd go to a motel afterward and she'd have to do it. I bet Biff was relieved!"—which, in fact, he was. The first night he and Ray Daniel McCullar, his cousin and best friend in Twiler, were able to get away and really get drunk at the Johnson family still, Biff said he'd gone along with Patsy Kay's plan only to maintain his prospects of eventually overseeing Sonny's land. Now he could keep that option intact and not have to worry about excuses to sneak out of the house to see Jessie Maynard. This was heard on good authority because Ray Daniel told his wife who worked at the beauty parlor in Twiler and she told Becky Smith's mama while she was visiting her sister there and having a permanent wave. Becky Smith's mama called Hally Jordan's mama while Hally was making a peanut butter sandwich (we had gotten hold of the Presley family recipe) and Hally heard everything on the kitchen extension.

The decision having been made that they would not get married, Patsy Kay wasn't about to waste all this time off from school, and besides, she had never been to Florida.

"I told Biff since Daddy was going to kill us anyway when we got back, I'd just as soon see Florida before I died!" Everyone laughed heartily, but I knew when she had said it to Biff in Georgia, they both knew it was only half in jest.

After the impromptu reception courtesy of Mr. Randolph, we all filed in, saw the flick, and followed the celebrated couple to Shug's Drive-In. Patsy Kay's dress never split, but we all enjoyed the suspense.

It seems Hortense was so distraught over the drastic action to which she and Sonny had driven Patsy Kay, that she for the first time in her life stood up to Sonny and his temper. No, she would not let him lock Patsy Kay in her room for the rest of her life and he would not have Biff lynched. Years ago Hortense had given up hope of ever getting married, and then one day right there in the grocery store the widowed Sonny had ambled over and asked her to have supper with him. Asked her right there at the meat counter over the brisket of beef. He took her to Brown's Cafe and didn't say much, but he was pleasant enough and took her straight home. She despaired that he wouldn't call her, so she invited him to her apartment for supper the next week and got ready for three days. Shortly thereafter they got married and she proceeded to try to get pregnant. She finally went to some doctors in Memphis who told her it was impossible. Six months later she discovered she was indeed with child and her joy knew no bounds.

Her little girl! She had dressed her in ruffles and bows from the day she came home from the clinic. When Patsy Kay started sucking her thumb and twirling her baby-fine hair, in a fruitless effort to stop her, a bow went around the twirl—but that was no more effective than the Tabasco, vinegar, and you-name-it in which the thumb had been dipped since. Patsy Kay was as hell bent about sucking her thumb then as she was about getting herself a man now. Hortense had taken Patsy Kay to Memphis to buy her Easter clothes. She had enrolled her in Miss Maude's kindergarten. She wasn't going to lose her now. If the couple ever came back, Sonny had better behave himself. He'd better welcome them with open arms. He would receive Biff as a son and offer him employment. Yes, he would, too, have that no-good skunk working for him and he would pay him a living wage, enough to support Patsy Kay in fine style, if he never worked a single day. He would give them one of the houses in Humphrey Place, a development Sonny had hurriedly put together for government workers when the construction started on the dam. He would give Patsy Kay a car. Did he hear that? Huh?

Never had Sonny seen Hortense like this. She had loved, honored, and obeyed him since the day they were married. Especially obeyed. She came home from the second-grade class she taught and had supper on the table for him when he came in. She washed his clothes, she darned his socks, she kept his house sparking clean. She had even borne him a son. Although Sonny thought Bubby Lee was more trouble than he was worth, at least he would carry on the family name; this was deemed very important since Jane Ann was the only child from his first marriage and his brother Bubba had no children. Hortense was thrilled to give birth again, but there would never be another moment in her life like that first time she saw her first baby, her baby girl, her Patsy Kay. She had even named Patsy Kay after her favorite singer, Patsy Cline, thinking Cline began with a K.

No, Sonny would do exactly as he was told, and that was that. And Sonny knew he would, too. He never again wanted to incur the wrath of Hortense Humphrey. Hortense was known far and wide for being a kind, good woman, a devoted member of the Enlightened Morning Star Baptist Church, a person who visited the sick and helped everyone whenever she could. She was loved by everyone in town. But his life had been hell from the minute they had left the principal's office. That, however, was a mute point now. Patsy Kay and Biff had not married. Sonny didn't have to shell out a thing except give Patsy Kay the car. Just let Patsy Kay go out with Biff. Just be nice to Biff. God! Sonny hoped that didn't include Sunday dinner!

Things were fairly quiet on that subject for a while so the hottest topic of conversation was Elizabeth Taylor's running off with Debbie Reynolds' husband. We discussed the matter thoroughly at Shug's, but the Enlightened Ladies were just thoroughly indignant. The way the situation was discussed at the bridge parties, you'd have thought the Debbie and Eddie Fisher lived down the street with Elizabeth's house being in Rolling Hills. With Elvis' serving our country out of the jurisdiction of Hollywood and the scandal so sensational, "Cat on a Hot Tin Roof" was the biggest moneymaker MGM had that year. (I personally tended to give Paul Newman the credit.)

We were, however, subjected to Patsy Kay's minute-by-minute account of every date she had with Biff. We were much more interested in Elizabeth Taylor but patiently endured the much-embellished details even after school was out for the summer and Patsy Kay was droning on about Biff even as we baked in the sun out at the dam. To get away from her constant chatter, Claudia stayed in the water so much she actually learned to swim! Patsy Kay and Biff kept going out until one night when she came in at four o'clock in the morning. That did it! Sonny blew his stack and was getting his gun out to do the same thing to Biff's empty head when Hortense woke up. When Sonny shouted the two could never see each other again (again), Patsy Kay strutted to her room, slammed the door, crawled out the window, and was in her new black Thunderbird convertible tooling down the highway to Twiler before daylight. She insisted Biff marry her that very day and that very day he did.

I don't think Hortense ever forgave Sonny. Even though he gave the newlyweds the house in Humphrey Place, bought them the furniture Hortense and Patsy Kay picked out in Memphis, had Mr. Hanks at the appliance store equip the whole kitchen, and even bought Patsy Kay a Steinway grand piano on which she could play nothing but "Chopsticks" despite the fact it took up most of the tiny living room. Hortense had been denied the big church wedding she had dreamed of for her little girl. Dreamed of for sixteen years. Why, she might even be denied Patsy Kay's high school graduation!

The Twelve dutifully honored Patsy Kay with The Shower, and we thought ourselves quite clever hostesses when our gift to the bride was a spoon (in the Sculptured Rose pattern) with a "12" engraved on the back. All the ladies in town came, mainly to see if Patsy Kay were showing—after all, they had heard Biff's sister had "been pregnant *twice* and hadn't *ever* been married." We teenagers had long since discounted Sheriff Brimley's report, as Teebo had confirmed that Biff had no sisters and we had all seen Biff at Shug's wearing his high school letter jacket. We used this occasion to delicately start spreading this truth before the next election.

Patsy Kay did continue to go to school and acted like a martyr that she was making this effort despite her wifely burdens. She acted very knowledgeable about sex and kept The Twelve in hysterics telling us each day about the soufflé that had exploded the night before. About how she spent three days making some spaghetti—we heard about all the pots, pans, and groceries this trial-and-error (mainly error) project expended, only to find out during one of her frequent slips of the tongue that what she cooked for three days was spaghettios. About how she had spent hours ironing Biff's shirts, which we knew very well all went to the Vincent Cleaners, because Teebo Vincent, who helped at his uncle's cleaners on Saturdays, reported, "She brings Biff's clothes in and I deliver them right back to her door. She hasn't ironed a shirt or anything else since they got hitched."

We saw Patsy Kay and Biff at Shug's every night, so the cooking and soufflé explosions did not take place for the evening meal. We also figured if their sex life were as spectacular as Patsy let on, she would have kept her mouth entirely shut.

Jimmie Gayle and Dex went to Memphis and returned with the report that Elvis had a girlfriend in Germany.

Becky

ABOUT THAT TIME The Twelve experienced another dropout—Becky Smith. Billy Hooper was three years older than The Twelve, but having been in the band, he was buddies with all us majorettes. When he went to the University he found himself rooming with Jerry Meadows from Kentucky. They would drive over in Jerry's new Ford all the time and one weekend Billy felt called upon to get Jerry a date. Becky was always dating older boys and had long blond hair and soulful blue eyes that made her look helpless. She was also known to put out, so Billy thought she would do just fine. Becky had just thrown Travis Dexter's class ring in his face when she caught him making out with Shelly Grayson, so Becky was free for the weekend. Her mama didn't say anything about her dating an older college man because she was so relieved to have Travis (the older generation would not call him "Dex") off her daughter's dance card. After Patsy Kay's trip to Georgia, no mama in town was about to forbid her daughter to see one of the local, church-going boys. Although Jerry did not fit into that category, Mrs. Smith had taught Billy in Sunday School his whole grammar school life, so it followed that his college roommate had to be a paragon of virtue.

Jerry continued to see Becky on the weekends. He was very impressed with Becky's well-formed breasts and especially impressed that she let him feel them. He was back the next night and took her straight to the reservoir to get to know her better. After that they could regularly be seen parked at Shug's late at night, and that was about all we saw of her outside of school. We thought it was very exciting that one of our number was dating an older college man from out of state.

One night Hally's daddy agreed to take some of us over to the University to watch Robert Mitchum film a movie. I was so excited I just couldn't *stand* it! When we got over there, Dr. Jordan let us out of the car and said he was going to the picture show. We were delighted, as Hally's mama had made him promise not to let us out of his sight! We called Billy Hooper. He arrived in his car, and Jerry Meadows arrived in his. All of us went with Billy except Becky.

Billy drove us around looking for Robert Mitchum. There were huge lighting setups everywhere, but no movie stars, no night shooting. We decided to go get a coke on campus, went to the cafe, and there with two other people was Robert Mitchum! My heart was pounding so hard, I was sure he could hear it clear across the room. Hally, wearing a flaming red coat that was so full it looked like a cloak, swooped over to his table like a vampire, screeched to a halt, and posed provocatively while she said about a five-syllabled, "Hi—iii-iiii—ii-iii!" as the rest of us swarmed his table like bees around a hive.

He looked up with those wonderful, half-closed eyes and said in that wonderful low voice, "Well, hello—oo-oo!"

He looked straight at me and held me in his gaze. Thud! *thud*, ***thud***! My heart was about to come out of my chest. My temples pounded. He didn't say anything about my heart. Maybe he hadn't heard it. Boom. *Boom.* ***Boom***!!!

I was so shocked at Hally's entrance, I didn't know what to say. He was with some friends, and I knew we shouldn't be interrupting. "May I have your autograph?" I asked lamely. I was very disappointed I hadn't been witty and clever—he'd heard the autograph thing a jillion times.

"Why, of course!" He smiled that great sleepy grin.

He was gracious to all of us. Courtly, in fact. He seemed tired and though we were intruding and acting like maniacs, he acted as though he were honored to have five silly little high school sophomores barge in on him.

We were all thrilled, and I've often reflected on how his kindness that night might have affected the rest of Hally's life.

One day the bombshell dropped that Becky and Jerry had been married for three months, so naturally the assumption was that Becky was at least two months pregnant. The Twelve hurriedly had to throw The Shower together, but Hally Jordan said confidently, "Don't worry about a thing. My mama can put on a party with her eyes closed and two hands tied behind her back," and the deed got done the next Saturday afternoon. No one except Hally had seen Becky since the news got out, but that was at Piggly Wiggly and when Hally stopped at the cantaloupes to talk to Becky and her mother a while.

"But I don't know if she's pregnant," Hally said, "Becky had on a great big sweater so I couldn't tell if she were showing."

At The Shower, Patsy Kay was trying to compare notes with Becky about their wedding nights but Becky kept changing the subject, even when

Patsy Kay said she'd kept Biff waiting on the nuptial bed for three hours while she took four baths. This was about the tenth version of her wedding night that Patsy Kay had confided, so we gave it as much credence as the soufflés. We really didn't care whether Becky ever said she was pregnant or not because we knew Patsy Kay would find out even if she had to go over to the University to investigate and bribe a lab technician. The baby, a little girl, was born six months later and Patsy Kay shot over to the University as fast as the T-Bird would fly so she could say she saw it first.

About six months after that, word got around that there was a peeping tom looking in various windows at night. He had first been seen by Betty Mae's mother from their den about ten o'clock the same night John August saw him looking in Martha Louise Potter's window about eleven-thirty. It got so some of the ladies felt left out if he hadn't been seen looking in their windows.

"I know good and well Mary Perkins lied when she said the peeping tom looked in her window on Wednesday night around eight o'clock," Sarah Jane commented, "because everybody knows Mary was at prayer meeting. She sat by Johnnie Kat's mama."

Sheriff Brimley cautioned the ladies who lived alone not to go out until "I catch that scumbag," and his deputies were kept busy checking out every evening phone call.

After about three months of this, one night the culprit was apprehended and the shocked population learned his identity.

"It's Jerry Meadows," Patsy Kay announced on the steps of the high school as we awaited the bell for school to start. Somehow she had found out the night before—maybe from a deputy who had gone by Shug's—"Becky rushed home from the University with her baby to be with her mama. I rushed over as soon as I heard, but she won't see anybody. You know she'd at *least* see *me* if she'd see *anybody*!"

"Yeah. Right," deadpanned Claudia as she picked some tobacco off her tongue. Claudia didn't join the guys in smoking behind the auditorium, as Malcolm P. Clovis periodically checked to see who was there. She knew Malcolm P. had gotten a real rush from the role he played in the Patsy Kay episode, and he would relish calling the prominent James Balfour Seaton at city hall to report the sins of his daughter.

That afternoon Teebo Vincent reported Becky had not gone over to the jail, and no one had put up Jerry's bail. Before too much time could be wasted in surveillance of the Smith home, however, Becky decided to be the noble wife and talked Calvin into going over and getting his new son-in-law out of the clink. The next day Becky called the town hotline and briefly told Patsy Kay she was going to stand by her man and they were going to his home in Kentucky to start over. His parents were going to get him a psychiatrist and he was going to go on to get his degree at the local college there. When Becky hung up, we knew she had been confident word would get around and she need not call anyone else. We never saw her again.

* * *

One Monday Jimmie Gayle and Dex did not come to school. This was noteworthy because no member of the football team would play hooky until after Thanksgiving and the selections for the all-conference team were final. Even Sallybeth had no idea where they were—she hadn't even seen Jimmie Gayle on Sunday.

During study hall the majorettes practiced.

"I tried to call Jimmie Gayle at lunch to see if he's sick," reported Sallybeth as the majorettes got lined up for drill, "and there was no answer. His mama didn't even come to the phone."

Then shockwaves went straight through those of us Teebo gathered at the pencil sharpener right before fourth-period history class—Jimmie Gayle Trambeau and Travis Dexter were in jail! Teebo had hurriedly assembled a few of us in the back of the classroom prior to Miss Greenway's arrival and whispered, "I went home at lunch. Duck was eating Myrtle's meatloaf," he began. Teebo treated his parents with the utmost respect, calling them "Mother" and "Dad"—but when referring to them, they were always "Myrtle" and "Duck."

"You know Duck tells Myrtle everything, and I overheard him say that Jimmie Gayle and Dex were caught out at Bubba Humphrey's rustling Bubba's cows. Instead of horses they used Jimmie Gayle's latest new car, and while Jimmie Gayle flew around the pasture driving the car, Dex was riding the fender tossing knives, using the cows for targets. When a cow went down, they supposedly cut out its heart." Supposedly they had four hearts lined up on the fence when they got caught.

"When Sheriff Brimley got there he was already mad as a banty rooster because Bubba woke him up and got him out of his nice, warm house, and seeing the bloody mess lit by the search lights wasn't gonna help him digest his catfish and hush puppies. His deputy's car had blocked the gate to the pasture, and even Jimmie Gayle wasn't gonna crash the stone fence on that side—his daddy would do worse than cut out his heart if he crashed his new car."

We were all flabbergasted.

"Being covered with blood didn't help any, so Sheriff Brimley carted them both off to jail."

Charles Trambeau was then summoned from *his* bed and after seeing the boys at the jail still in their blood-stained clothes, he refused to take them home. He stood there ever silent, looming in the doorway to the jail cells, turned around, and stormed out the front door. He would just teach them a lesson and see them at the hearing on Monday. When he got home he assured Charlene the boys were fine in Sheriff Brimley's care and then went back to bed.

Teebo added, "The guys probably felt safer in jail anyway than home with what Charles might do to them once they got there."

Teebo had never heard Charles say anything either, but he was a huge red-faced man viewed as the *especially* strong, silent type and the kind *no* one would want to tangle with.

While Teebo delivered this shocking report we all stood there dumbfounded. Although we hardly knew Dex, I just could not *believe* Jimmie Gayle would do such a thing.

"I don't think Jimmie Gayle did it," I stated emphatically.

Hally was a little skeptical, "Maybe the hoped-for rehabilitation worked in reverse."

I was indignant, "We all know Jimmie Gayle. We've known him all our lives. And you know how he loves animals. He's about as bad as you are, Hally, about bringing strays home. Sure, he's the Toilet Paper King, but he'd never hurt an animal. Teebo—let's keep this quiet—there's something else going on here."

Teebo agreed. Claudia solemnly observed, "'Innocent until proven guilty' is what Perry Mason would say." Claudia *loved* Raymond Burr. I was waiting for her to work in, "Incompetent, irrelevant, and immaterial."

Hally looked thoughtful, "He had blood all over his clothes!"

Claudia didn't miss a beat—"Incompetent, irrelevant, and immaterial!"

"Okay. Let's make a pact," Hally declared. "Let's keep this quiet until we know for sure what happened."

Teebo nodded. "We owe Jimmie Gayle that." We all placed our hands one on top of another and shook. We felt virtuous.

"We have to do something about Patsy Kay," I said.

"Now *that's* a tall order! We'll just have to play it by ear," Teebo laughed. "Give me a little time and I'll get this all straight. You girls take care of Patsy Kay." We agreed, but we had no idea how to throw Patsy off the trail or how long it would take her to find out the rumor, but we would try to keep her occupied at least until after the hearing—no small feat. Claudia volunteered to invite her to go smoke after school—that would keep her sequestered and away from Shug's.

Neither boy was at school the next day either. There was a rumor that jail was involved, but it could not be confirmed even by Patsy Kay, who in order to keep the spotlight, held court wondering aloud if we were safe around Jimmie Gayle and Dex.

"We have never known why Dex had to leave Seattle," she pointed out.

"Patsy Kay," I countered, "you've known Jimmie Gayle Trambeau your whole life. He's always been nice to you—he's a perfect gentleman."

"Good honk, Margie!" Patsy Kay retorted. "You'd take up for an axe murderer as long as he had good manners!"

Hally changed the subject and asked Patsy Kay if she had been up to Graceland to see Elvis' uncle at the gate lately. We knew she hadn't but we also knew Patsy Kay had not heard of Teebo's report because she would have broadcast the details upon receipt.

"No," responded Patsy Kay, "but I need to see if Elvis's written a letter from Germany lately. I get to read his letters, you know."

"Yeah. Right," Claudia rolled her eyes to heaven.

Hally played along.

Then Patsy Kay said, "I'm fixing to go to Shug's after school"—whereupon Claudia, in an inspired moment, invited Patsy Kay to go smoking again, dangling the enticement, "I'll teach you how to blow smoke rings." Patsy Kay jumped at the chance, knowing Claudia was the best smoker around. Her smoke rings were works of art, and Patsy Kay was an ardent admirer. Hally and I ran in the girls restroom to laugh.

When Jimmie Gayle and Dex appeared on Wednesday, they acted as though nothing had happened. Teebo could get no more information from more rare appearances at his mother's table for the noon meal during the next two days (Tuesday—fried chicken, turnip greens, cornbread, and black-eyed peas—which we knew he hated; Wednesday—lima beans, beets, and more cornbread with liver and onions—Teebo was valiant indeed) or hanging around his dad at the court house after school—but he did overhear Duck tell Myrtle there had been a lot of secret goings-on between someone at the court house and Sheriff Brimley. We assumed Patsy Kay was afraid to ask the jailbirds why they had been incarcerated because she continued to speculate and wonder aloud about our safety.

Jimmie Gayle and Dex went on to football practice and the rest of their lives. They continued to go to church, wear their blue suede shoes, and Jimmie Gayle continued to pick me up when he would see me walking to town. What was strange was Bubba started driving a brand new Cadillac and Jimmie Gayle became an Honor Roll student. Dex didn't make the Honor Roll, but he stopped making D's and F's. He even made a B in history the day he made All Conference. He also yawned a lot. Someone did say he saw someone who looked like Dex covered with manure coming out of one of Bubba's barns late one night, but he wasn't really that close and of course Jimmie Gayle's cousin would never be cleaning a barn.

One day Teebo called another meeting at the pencil sharpener. He had just suffered through Myrtle's string bean casserole, but his mission had finally met with success.

"That Saturday night Jimmie Gayle was going to take Sallybeth home and then meet Dex at Shug's," Teebo began breathlessly. "Dex didn't show up so Jimmie Gayle went cruising to find him. He'd seen the car Charles had loaned Dex parked on the edge of Bubba's property and went to investigate. When he found Dex had slaughtered a cow, he'd tried to stop him. They had a terrible fight and Bubba heard the ruckus and had called the sheriff. When the sheriff showed up, Jimmie Gayle's clothes were covered in blood from all the blood on Dex's clothes. Jimmie Gayle wouldn't rat on Dex, so both of 'em went to jail. At the hearing on Monday, Dex confessed and cleared Jimmie Gayle. And it was only one cow."

This bit of intelligence came to light none too soon—Myrtle had already planned to serve broccoli with chicken and dumplings for dinner the next day.

"Dex was supposedly sentenced to hard labor at Bubba's, but since Bubba wants Addison to be conference champions, Dex is to serve his time after football practice and on weekends." Bubba had also apparently made it clear Dex had better do his part every Friday night from the kickoff. We had Trey Justice (another The Third) for a quarterback and if we were ever going to make state champions, this was the time.

One hot afternoon the next summer I was walking to band practice and Jimmie Gayle came up alongside. He tooted the horn and I got in.

"Open the glove compartment," he said. I thought I was probably going to give him a pen or something. I opened it and there was a beautifully wrapped present inside.

"Take that out. It's for you," Jimmie Gayle said matter-of-factly.

"What!! I—I—why?" I gasped.

"Open it." Jimmie Gayle never took his eyes off the road.

I took out the box, which had the gold Goldsmith's sticker on it. It had shiny gold paper and a white silk ribbon. I opened it and unwrapped the tissue. Inside was a gleaming gold compact engraved with my initials. I was flabbergasted!

"Jimmie GAYLE!" I squealed. "What on earth—!" I turned the compact over and in small letters was engraved, "Thanks—JGT."

"I heard what you did for me. You and Claudia and Hally and Teebo. Just keeping your mouths shut and not helping that rumor get around would have been enough, but you believed in me—that was important. And you really took up for me when it came up at Shug's and you were the one who got the others to stand by me." Then he grinned, "And keeping Patsy Kay at bay—WOW!! That really took some work!"

I laughed—"I think even Claudia got her fill of smoking! She's still threatening to quit! But Jimmie Gayle, this is too much. You know I'd take up for you. And you'd do the same for me."

He became serious. "Well, I know you spoke up for me first and got the others lined up on my side. I'll never forget what you did. I promise. And if you ever need anything—ever—just let me know. For the rest of your life."

I reached out and touched his hand on the steering wheel. "Thank you. It's a beautiful gift, and I'll treasure it."

Jimmie Gayle took great pride in his mischief like the toilet-paper rolling but always shunned thank-yous and absolutely could not cope with compliments. He abruptly changed the subject.

"I'm glad y'all are having band practice again. Sallybeth was at majorette camp at the University for two weeks. Daddy lets me use the cars, but I have to pay the gas bills. By the way, did you hear what happened with Nicki Love?"

I hadn't yet seen Sallybeth, our feature twirler, so the tales of her encounters with Nicki Love from Pontotoc, her chief rival at state twirling competitions, had yet to be told. "No! What happened?" I was dying to know.

"Well," began Jimmie Gayle, "a lot of the girls had heard of Sallybeth and of course a lot of girls around the state know her from the twirling contests, so when they heard she had checked into the dorm, they started coming over to her room. She was sitting there holding court and the girls were catching up, when in walked Nicki Love.

"She sailed in like the Queen of Sheba and said, 'Hello, Everybody, I'm Nicki Luvvvv. My fahtha's Senatuh Luvvvvv—' Before she could say anything else high and mighty, Sallybeth got up and held out her hand and went over to greet her like she'd never met her before and said, 'Well, helloooo! My name is Sallybeth Waltrip. *My* fahtha is Virgie Waltrip, owner of Virgie Waltrip's Last-chance Gas, Minnows and Worms!'"

Good ol' Sallybeth—she not only beat the senator's snooty daughter at all the twirling contests, she had blown away her standard opening line in front of the foremost majorettes in the state! Since this occurred the first day of majorette camp, the rest of the majorettes state-wide immediately heard about that encounter, and Sallybeth got congratulatory mail until way up around homecoming. One letter even came from the Gulf Coast. That year at school Nicki Love quit the band and became a cheerleader. Her daddy lost the next election.

About this time Bubba and Della Humphrey were killed in a car wreck. Everybody knew Sarah Jane Mosely's mama, Jane Ann, was Bubba's favorite niece, and since the couple had no children, Jane Ann inherited everything. Everything. All the land, all the money, the cars, and the house out on the Dam Road. The only catch was that she had to live in the house. This was not seen as a problem, what with the house being one of those great southern mansions with the white columns and all—Jane Ann would just love being the mistress of the manor. And there was so much money involved in the estate that there would be enough for her to fix up the house any way she wanted, even after she and Sarah Jane had gone to Memphis and outfitted themselves at Goldsmith's, Gerber's, *and* Lowenstein's. They placed a big gate at the large circular drive, but I didn't care, as by that time I knew how to back up.

I was actually glad Sarah Jane had some running-around money. I'll never forget the time she and I were out at Shug's before Patsy Kay's The Shower.

"I don't know what I'm gonna do!" she confided.

"What do you mean, S'erJane?" I responded. Sarah Jane was not one to confide in me very often, as Patsy Kay was her aunt and she usually told her all her secrets. Which was how we all knew what they were.

"Well, my mama told me I had to pay for the centerpiece out of my own money, and I don't have any! I spent it all on that bottle of "Evening in Paris" last week. She still thinks I helped Patsy Kay out some way. She just won't believe I had nothing to do with it."

"I can't help you out—I don't have any money either—Mother said she'd help me out on this one," I responded.

"I'll be humiliated if I can't contribute my part! *Ruined*!!" I could tell Sarah Jane was desperate.

She turned on the ignition and scratched off, wheeling around Shug's like one of the guys. Then she started up the highway.

"Riding around helps me think," she allowed. "There must be something I can do."

She lit up a cigarette and blew the smoke out the window. We cut through the town square and drove up by the Presbyterian Church. We kept on going toward the cemetery, and suddenly Sarah Jane turned in. I didn't think much of this, as we had a beautiful cemetery and it was not unusual for anyone to drive through it. People were constantly placing flowers on the well-tended graves, and family members frequently came to give a look-see to the family plots. It was a lovely, bright day, and the marble of the tombstones gleamed in the sun. The carpet of grass was perfectly cut and looked soft and restful on the gently rolling hills. The grandparents I never knew were buried over by the oak tree. The flowers on the graves were bursting with color.

We were driving unusually slowly for Sarah Jane. She was eyeing the graves closely.

"Maybe there are some around here," she said with determination.

"Some what?"

"Flowers, of course."

"Flowers?" I couldn't imagine—

"Flowers for Patsy Kay's shower," Sarah Jane replied. "I can just use some of these."

"S'erJane! You couldn't! You *wouldn't*!" I exclaimed in disbelief. This was low, even for Sarah Jane.

Sarah Jane kept the Pontiac creeping along the small drive around the family plots. "Who got buried last week? No, those flowers would be too old. Maybe somebody just came and felt like putting down some flowers for a birthday or something. Or I could call the funeral home and ask—Ol' Miz Crouch has been real sick at the clinic—"

"S'erJane!" I was horrified. I looked at my watch. Fortunately it was almost six o'clock. "We have to go, S'erJane—you said you'd pick up Sallybeth—remember?"

"Oh, yeah. I forgot," Sarah Jane said as she turned the car toward the front gate of the cemetery. I was relieved her grave-robbing career had been cut short. Surely she'd just talk her mother into helping her. Sarah Jane could talk her mother into anything.

The next day I arrived at Hally's house for The Shower about an hour ahead of time since I was one of The Twelve and co-hosting. Hally and her mama had to leave on a last-minute errand, so I went to see to last-minute details. I opened the side door that led to the kitchen—I was bringing my beloved cokes. The food was still in the kitchen in the fridge. The presents were laid out neatly in the living room and all the cards were showing just so. Hally's mama was remarkable. I went into the dining room and there was the crystal punch bowl and all the cups, sparkling and bright. And there was the centerpiece, a circle of purple satin covered with pink carnations. During The Shower I heard a number of compliments about the unusual arrangement. No one realized it was a wreath. Not even Mrs. Dulaney, at whose mother's grave it had stood the day before.

One day when I answered my telephone, Claudia began with "Have you seen *The Addisonian?*"

"No, we haven't gotten our mail yet," I answered.

"Well, Miss Whitley got hers this morning. You know they're doing a series of articles on Civil War heroes of this area and various ancestors—"

"Oh, yeah," I recalled, "They started with James T. Addison and told all about his exploits and about Letitia and Bonnie's family being descendants. Then they told about Hally's family—Miz Blanche's folks and all. They're going do this 'til we run out of Civil War relatives. That ought to take up space well into the next century."

"Not if Miss Whitley sues them and they go bankrupt!"

"Whaaat?" My curiosity was aroused.

"There's a misprint in an article in today's issue on Miss Whitley's grandfather. Supposedly he was some sort of hero somewhere during the War but in the write-up they said he was a 'battle *scared* veteran'—she's already called John David Farrell about suing for defamation or slander or something. She's mad as a wet hen and having a hissyfit!"

We burst into laughter. How many hours had we had to sit in Miss Whitley's class and hear how her ancestors had practically single-handedly won every victory the South achieved! Somehow she managed to have an ancestor at every major battle and they all should have gotten the Confederate equivalent of Congressional Medal of Honor. It had long before gotten to the point that we took her stories with a grain of salt—about like we took Patsy Kay's—but we still were captive audiences as she spun the tales. We could recite them word for word as she told them. I had never forgiven her for making me read *The Deerslayer* for a book report. She'd made Terry read *Wuthering Heights*. We were both dying and went to her with the request that we could at least swap. We fully expected her to okay the deal, but she would not. I had to read vivid descriptions about scalpings and he had to endure what he termed a "nauseating love story." As far as I was concerned, she deserved whatever she got, even at the expense of her long-dead grandfather.

"How fantastic!" I squealed. "She's getting some come-uppance!"

"This ought to be interesting," Claudia resumed. "She just called my momma and kept her on the phone for an hour. I could hear her every time I passed through the room. She's fit to be tied!"

Miss Whitley continued to call everyone in town and carry on. It was Jimmie Gayle's toilet paper scenario all over again. We were snickering about it at Shug's, at Sunday School, in study hall—we were filled with glee. Someone asked if Jimmie Gayle had sneaked over to *The Addisonian* and set the type.

John David Farrell, ever the diplomat, worked out a retraction with the editor, and Miss Whitley was promised that it would be printed on the front page of the very next edition of *The Addisonian*. We had a relatively quiet weekend, and then the paper came out again.

"Did you see the retraction?" Claudia began her phone conversation.

"No—is the crisis over?" I was sorry it had taken only a week.

"Probably not. They printed an apology and re-printed the article. Now Miss Whitley's grandfather is a '*bottle* scarred veteran!' Isn't that just too much!"

Miss Whitley didn't come to school the rest of the week. We heard she had taken to her bed over Grandpa Whitley, now the town's famous drunken coward.

My faith in the press had been restored. It had been quite shaken when I heard the *New York Times* had said that rock'n'roll was a communicable disease.

Johnnie Kat

WE WERE ALL surprised when Johnnie Kat Botty was elected homecoming queen. She was one of The Twelve, but she did not date any of the football players—although she *did* smoke a lot and Trey Justice was her cousin. She was constantly criticizing everybody's manners and getting away with it without being told *that* was bad manners. One time while we were planning a party, Sallybeth made a suggestion and was accused by Johnnie Kat of being "rural." To this very day, whenever Johnnie Kat is absent from the group, someone works in how "rural" someone else is just so they can all titter about it. But we went on and helped decorate her float and told her how pretty her gosh-awful evening dress that made her look pregnant was, and she had a successful reign all night long. Terry had to be her escort across the football field and when he first saw the dress before the afternoon homecoming parade, he gasped, "I hope nobody thinks I'm the father!"

Though she and I subsequently went to different colleges, the thirty-mile distance between us allowed her to come to visit me on the weekends as a refuge from the strict religious atmosphere she had to endure throughout the week. Late one Friday afternoon she called at the last minute when I had plans for the whole weekend to ask if she could come to stay until Sunday. I told her I wouldn't be around, but she said she didn't care, she just wanted off that righteous campus. After she had arrived, she and I went to the student union to meet my boyfriend and his roommate to play bridge. As we played, Beau Hillsbreath, an upperclassman whom I had met my first day at the school and now one of my best friends, after kibitzing a few minutes, asked to see me privately while Eric dealt the new hand. Beau asked if he could take Johnnie Kat out that night. "Please!" I exclaimed, relieved as he removed my guilt at leaving her in the dorm alone. They hit it off immediately and the week after I graduated from college, I was an attendant in their wedding, the biggest event Addison had seen in years. As members of The Twelve swept down the aisle of the Enlightened Morning Star Baptist Church, I expected Ed Sullivan to come out to announce the next act.

We were lovely girls in lilac dresses "full length to the floor," carrying lilacs, of which our headdresses were also made, wearing lilac dyed-to-match satin pumps. That afternoon our hair had to be combed by Lucy Jones, the beautician of the month—the latest local graduate of a beauty school in Memphis who had come home to make her fortune. She had opened shop in the vacant store next to the pool hall. I walked in to the shop to get beautified for the nuptials and found myself in a bower of calla lilies. Calla lilies were everywhere. At the entrance, on each counter, to the side of each mirror. There was a pot of calla lilies at the wash basins. Lucy was expected to know the latest techniques of fashion pulchritude and make us all look like movie stars. When she finished with *my* movie-star look, I thought she must have confused me with the bride—the Bride of Frankenstein. I was mortified! I placed a scarf over my horrified head "to keep the wind off"—mainly so I wouldn't be utterly humiliated in front of the entire town of Addison. There was no hurricane that would have made the sprayed mass on my head move. I ducked out the back. Those calla lilies had thrown me off guard.

Later at the church, before appearing to precede Johnnie Kat down the aisle, I clandestinely fled to a vacant Sunday School room and recombed the sculpture, no mean feat in view of the hairspray which lay dying on the teased brown tresses of my head. Lucy had sentenced the long black hair of Hally Jordan to endure the same fate, so Hally joined me in this secret operation which we concealed right up to the point that Connie Lou Rattermier, the PiKA Dreamgirl who, as noted in the weekly *Addisonian*, had come all the way from Corinth, sang *Because*. Hally and I then scooted into line and took our places under the scathing gaze of Johnnie Kat as the Lilac Ladies step-paused to the alter.

But we had quite a wait to whisk ourselves into line. Miss Alma played the organ preliminaries right up to the point that we were supposed to get ready to march down to get the deed done. Then she started over and played all the wedding music again. Then she started up the third time. Hally and I were concerned from our hiding place in the Sunday School room that we were being sought out, and although we had heard a siren at the beginning of the second medley, no one had appeared to be leaving the church. When Sallybeth waltzed by during the second run-through, we learned that we had not even been missed. In the rush to get the Wedding of the Century so perfect, so many details were seen to that no one thought to order the bride a bouquet. This became apparent only when the bridesmaids got their posies at the church and there were none for the bride. Sachet Biggs was recalled from her seat on the aisle and ushered into the room with Johnnie Kat and her fuming mother. God knows the Wedding of the Century could not take place without a bridal bouquet, and Sachet Biggs knew it too, in no uncertain terms as delivered by Katheryn Botty, Mother of the Bride.

"*You* were responsible for all the flowers for this wedding, Sachet," bellowed Mrs. Botty. "You didn't even have the sense to put the most important flowers together!"

"I was responsible for what was *ordered*," retorted Sachet. "No one *ordered* a bride's bouquet. I thought that Beau was probably providing it from someone else!"

"*Who* else, you idiot," yelled Katheryn Botty, "you're the only florist in town!"

"Don't call me an idiot, you idiot! You are the first mama I ever heard of dumb enough not to order her daughter a *bouquet*!"

A catfight was about to ensue when Johnnie Kat just screamed, "Will you two stop this hollering this *minute*! Just *somebody* get me some flowers! If you don't I swear I'll light up a cig and smoke it down the aisle. The music is playing!"

A horrified silence hit the scene, as Katheryn Botty and everbody else knew Johnnie Kat was not bluffing. She was furious.

Sachet was then dispatched over to the florist shop she managed, Flowers by Squench, by Sheriff Brimley in his squad car to quickly put together the Bouquet of the Century. She knew Katheryn Botty would never stand for white carnations, so she split her two precious white orchids and wired them around a plastic magnolia that she hoped the mother of the bride wouldn't spot until after her darling daughter was safely married. Caught beforehand Katheryn Botty would probably say the marriage performed with plastic flowers would be illegal—certainly not sanctioned by the church. Sachet further camouflaged the garland with baby's breath and flew out to the chief law-enforcement officer of Addison who was primed to hit the siren once again.

Upon their arrival, a relieved and exhausted Miss Alma got the signal and told Connie Lou to take her last sip from the cup of honey and tea hiding behind the gladiolus and raise her voice in joyous song.

As I passed Patsy Kay, who was on the aisle straining to see while the husband at her side, hair coated for the occasion with Vaseline, dressed up in his Sunday-go-to-meetin' suit, stared down at his hands, I knew if Patsy Kay had known her impulsive act would have taken her out of consideration as a Lilac Lady in the most talked-about and celebrated event of the year, and more important, out of The Twelve, she would never have gunned that Thunderbird to Twiler. She was not only excluded from this solemn processional, but also not invited to the Bridesmaids' Luncheon and knew exceedingly well that what was discussed over the trout almandine was anyone who wasn't there.

We were expected to attend each and every to-do wearing a sheath dress, high-heeled shoes, gloves, and a hat. Pearls were recommended but optional. I could not stand wearing hats, but dutifully found some little hats which were mostly net and gave them a shot. At the umpteenth bridge party we were served our umpteenth lime sherbet. I looked through the veil down at the dessert which I was supposed to eat while thusly veiled and picked up my spoon. I looked through the veil across the table to Sallybeth who was looking back at me through hers. "This is enough of this foolishness," I declared. I took off my hat as audible gasps were heard from the next bridge table.

"I'm not eating another bite through a veil or while I have on a hat. Never. In my whole life."

Sallybeth giggled and leaned forward. "You may never be invited to another bridge party again! Or luncheon. Or wedding!"

I was resolute. "I don't care. Great! I will never wear a hat again unless it's functional—like a sunhat in the middle of the desert or something. I wore the gloves over here. That ought to count for something. I'm surprised we're not expected to wear them while we deal the cards!"

Sallybeth started her laugh-covering cough which was perfected during her posse ride to Twiler. People probably thought she was as sick as our friend Teebo, the coughing, drink-of-water addict.

The church was filled beyond capacity, and the wedding party also included a lot of the friends from college that Beau, Connie Lou, and I shared. Johnnie Kat had been given more lunches and bridal showers than we could count on both hands—as various waistlines could attest. The Shower plus a kitchen shower, a linen shower, several bridge parties, the luncheons, several coffees—as newlyweds, she and Beau were more prepared for housekeeping than most Addisonians that had been married for many years. Johnnie Kat's father, campaign manager for two successful gubernatorial candidates and therefore a very wealthy insurance executive, had gifted the couple with a new car and a gas credit card for which he would pay the bill until Beau had graduated from medical school, which Beau had found unbelievably easy to enter (another gift from Johnnie Kat's father which went unmentioned) once his engagement to Johnnie Kat had been announced in the major newspapers throughout the South.

Johnnie Kat came down the aisle on her daddy's arm and you could just hear the ooh's and aaah's at the sight—she was worth the wait. It had been widely publicized that her veil had originally come from Belgium and been in the family for four generations. She arrived at the altar and we all turned to face the preacher, Brother Fox. He started one of his long-winded speeches about the rings being symbols of the never-ending circle of love. He droned on about how serious the commitment was. He kept on going in high gear about Beau and Johnnie Kat and their Beginning as One.

Claudia leaned over and whispered through her lilacs, "After all the pre-game shows, I'd like to think of this as an *Ending*."

We were all exhausted after all the pre-wedding festivities. Now we were nearing the finish line. Then one of Beau's groomsmen ran over and stood behind him. The startled preacher actually stopped in mid-sentence, but ever the actor, he knew the show must go on. I looked at Beau. His eyes were closed and he seemed to be wavering, rocking back and forth. The best man stepped forth and grabbed Beau's arm, holding him up at his shoulder. Johnnie Kat shot Beau a concerned look. Beau's knees buckled. The groomsman steadied him, but Brother Fox didn't miss a beat. I could see Beau was fixing to go down.

Beau did indeed hit the floor. The other groomsmen rushed to his aid while Johnnie Kat coiled back in horror.

"Daddy!" she squealed. There was giggling on the third row. The Enlightened Ladies held their collective breath.

Beau was fanned and patted and his hands were rubbed. He sat up and insisted he could continue. The ceremony resumed. Brother Fox did not prudently hurry things along and pronounce them man and wife, but backtracked and rehashed the whole Neverending Circle business.

There was an audible THUNK. Beau was lying face up, eyes closed and spreadeagled at his wedding bower. The groomsmen, like efficient pallbearers, scooped him up and carried him out.

Johnnie Kat refused to leave the altar. She wouldn't even go to sit with the parents of the bride. She just kept saying "Oh, Daddy!" over and over. Her daddy put his protective arms around her and kept saying, "There, there."

The battalion of Lilac Ladies felt at loose ends, to say the least. We didn't know if Beau were backing out, drunk, or dying. This was one time Patsy Kay could not be called in for reconnaissance. Having been to college with Beau, I personally knew he could drink for days and still make it to chapter meeting. No dying there. The best man reappeared and informed that Beau would be joining us shortly. Beau sheepishly walked in looking weak. Johnnie Kat insisted an adjustment in the altar setup be made—she was not leaving to chance that Beau would depart the church a single man. The ceremony resumed. There were thousands of wedding pictures taken, but my favorite was taken from the back of the church looking up the aisle to the altar as Johnnie Kat and Beau exchanged their vows. There are Johnnie Kat and Beau in the Wedding of the Century sitting in scarred and creaking folding chairs stamped with "Acme Rentals." Yes, the nuptials of Johnnie Kat Botty had been worth the wait.

As it happened, the medical school which Beau attended was in New Orleans, beginning the September after I moved there in August to work in its finest hotel. We didn't know anyone else, and the three of us spent much happy time together getting to know the city ("Royal Street crosses Canal Street and then becomes St. Charles Avenue like in Monopoly and when it makes the 'L' it becomes Carrollton Avenue like the one at home") and its unique customs (such as decorating for Halloween—even lighting the roofs of houses—just as people in our home town decorated for Christmas. If Mr. Throckmorton had known, I was certain he would have moved bag and baggage to New Orleans.) We spent our first Mardi Gras together—the parades of the mystick krewes beat the hell out of anything we'd ever seen at Cotton Carnival in Memphis! We discovered people in New Orleans ate breakfast, lunch, and dinner—all our lives we'd eaten breakfast, dinner, and supper. New Orleans ate supper at 2:00 a.m. after a Mardi Gras Ball, and sometimes on Sunday they'd throw in something else called brunch. It seemed everyone in New Orleans was always waiting for the next meal.

After Johnnie Kat and Beau returned to Addison, we had lost touch except when they wanted to come to New Orleans on the sold-out football weekends and they called me to get them a free room and their party of ten in the premier restaurants that had long since stopped taking reservations. Johnnie Kat's father had set up Beau's medical offices, and shortly thereafter Beau's father died leaving Beau, the only son, real estate holdings which consisted of some buildings in Harrisville and the rent derived therefrom.

So when The Old Draper House went up for sale, there was plenty of money to buy it and fix it up as befitted the couple's expected high station in life. Once The Old Draper House was renovated and Beau and Johnnie Kat had moved in, the traditional surprise housewarming was held, before which Johnnie Kat made lists of gifts she wanted and dealt them to the merchants in town the day after she and Beau moved in. This would save time in the long run since she would have to spend less time returning "all those tacky gifts for credit."

From that day forward any relatives Johnnie Kat had with children getting married eagerly awaited her call offering the grand setting for The Shower, "provided of course no red punch or anything with blueberries is served." God forbid something might fall to the floor and fatally wound her carpets. No alcohol was *ever* served in the home as far as Johnnie Kat's mama was aware, as she was a leader in the Enlightened Morning Star Baptist Church. She did not know Beau's proudest renovation was a bar which revolved from behind a huge bookcase at the touch of a button pressed in his mother-in-law's absence. It was the envy of all his golfing buddies at the country club, especially since they lived in a dry county and all this alcohol Beau bought in Memphis was in his home illegally. Illegal booze in the Old Draper House.

Lena Sue

THE OLD DRAPER House had originally belonged to Mr. and Mrs. Thaddeus P. Draper. Mr. Draper owned Draper's Drygood Store, which sold mainly ladies dresses. After the Drapers died, Jim and Sadie Crawford (the Drapers' granddaughter) and their three children had moved in. Jim had been managing Draper's since Mr. Draper retired. Everyone was shocked when Jim Crawford committed suicide, but not for long. It got out that when little Johnny Grant came by to collect for his newspaper route, Sadie had gone looking for a check in Jim's desk and found a year-old deed to a cabin at the reservoir along with a canceled check for the down payment signed by Carol Ann Chimes. When Jim came home Sadie confronted him with the evidence, and Jim confessed he and Carol Ann had been carrying on at the cabin all that time—he really hadn't been fishing every Thursday afternoon, and all that trout and bass and perch he brought home came from Virgie Waltrip's Last-chance Gas, Minnows and Worms. Upon cleansing his conscience, he went upstairs and shot himself. Upon hearing the shot, Sadie gathered up the children and went to her mother's, never entering the house again. So there it stood all those years, dark and empty.

The home in which some Drapers actually *lived* was in the next block on Carrollton Avenue. When Sadie had moved back from The Old Draper House to her mother's, she and her sister (who had never moved out) had planted azaleas—white and rose-colored ones, all along the front of the house and down the long sidewalk to the street. They carefully tended the flowers and each year everyone anticipated the glorious array of color bursting forth from the perfectly symmetrical design. Everyone in town knew the sisters would get the "Yard of the Month" and the highly-prized Garden Club sign would be displayed by the front sidewalk. So gorgeous were the flowers that the sisters installed a timer for spotlights to snap on at sunset when the magnificent azaleas were in bloom, and in the soft spring night hundreds of cars slowly drove bumper-to-bumper down Carrollton Avenue. We knew for a fact that people came from as far away as Memphis, Clarksdale, and Tupelo. Some of us would go over to Bonnie and Letitia's house and sit in the big swing on their porch to watch the procession and little Johnny Grant selling lemonade at the end of the driveway. Why, the whole thing was featured in a Sunday edition of the Memphis *Commercial Appeal*, which was also the local daily newspaper for the northern part of the state, to include Addison.

The famous azaleas were the most exciting thing that had happened in the family since Jim's suicide—until Sadie's older daughter got married. This was going to be a Big Deal—probably the biggest since Beau and Johnnie Kat got married. Lena Sue was not only one of The Twelve, she was going to marry the most handsome boy in our high school graduating class, Andrew Jackson Brumfield, first chair trumpet, greatly admired by Tacawaw Henry. Everyone knew they would live happily ever after because Andy had just gotten his master's from State, had gotten his CPA, and was working for a big accounting firm in Memphis.

Preparations went on for months, and Lena Sue actually had more showers than Johnnie Kat. We bridesmaids got fitted a couple of times and finally the big day arrived. By early Sunday afternoon we were dutifully among the calla lilies at the salon of Lucy Jones as was customary—she was still the reigning beautician—before the evening nuptials, when Elsie Brumfield called for a bodywrap. Although she was the mother of the groom, the bodywrapper told Elsie she was doing a total wax job on Lena Sue's cousin which would take up her time the rest of the afternoon.

"You don't understand," wailed a tearful Elsie in desperation, "this is an *emergency!*" None of us had ever heard of an emergency bodywrap. Lucy herself went to the telephone to inquire what circumstance had transpired to elevate a bodywrap to such a vital plateau.

"I've been to so many coke parties and luncheons and bridge parties honoring the couple, that I've gained weight since the day I tried on my mother-of-the-groom gown. I can't get it fastened! I don't have anything else to wear! You *have* to help me," begged Elsie. "The wedding is in a matter of *hours!*" Elsie was indeed in despair.

Lucy told Elsie to hold, and everyone upon hearing Elsie's plight was totally sympathetic though in total hysterics, and leaped to help—even the aforementioned cousin—"Don't mind me—you just take Elsie and get her skinny enough to get into her dress. Elsie made soup for my mama when she was sick with the flu last year. I'll just shave my legs and come back next week." Lucy told Elsie to come right over to be rescued. "It wouldn't do for the mother of the groom not to be able to attend her own son's wedding."

The occasion was going to be at the Enlightened Morning Star Baptist Church and the reception would be at the country club, so tradition would be served. Or so everyone thought. What no one had counted on was Lena Sue had not selected the traditional *O Promise Me* and *Because* for her wedding music. When Miss Alma began playing the organ, the sensitive ears of the people of Addison were assaulted by songs from then-current Hollywood soundtracks. A murmur went through the shocked congregation starting with the quiet strains of *Moon River* and *Moonglow* right through the lighting of the candles accompanied as it was by *More.* When Elsie Brumfield (resplendent in her clinging mauve lace dress, thanks to the generosity of the Total Waxee) and Sadie, whose how-to-do was by now highly suspect despite her well-entrenched old-guard roots, were seated during *A Summer Place* and the show began, Miss Thelma Swango was close to cardiac arrest. To add insult to injury, no one sang a solo. Not even *I Love You Truly.* We bridesmaids who had practiced without music swept down the aisle to *A Place for Us* but thank God the bridal march finally and mercifully then began and Uncle Ross came down the center aisle with Lena Sue on his arm.

But if the Enlightened Ladies, who were all seated on the side of the bride since the family of Andrew Jackson Brumfield were Methodists, thought they would have nothing else to talk about tomorrow morning, they had another think coming. When she arrived at the altar, Lena Sue said she had something she wanted to say before the service began. The surprised minister nodded, Uncle Ross stepped aside, and Lena Sue turned to face those assembled. We of The Twelve just looked at each other in great suspense.

"I want to thank everyone for coming to share the happiest day of my life. I know many of you came from far away. I want to thank my mother for giving me this beautiful wedding and I want to thank all of you who entertained me and gave me such beautiful gifts. I want to thank my friends who are standing here today attending me as bridesmaids. But I especially want to thank my fiancé, Andrew Jackson Brumfield, and my maid of honor, Josephine Kennedy, for spending the night together last night instead of waiting until after I was married to this two-timing, no-good son-of-a-bitch!"

With that Lena Sue slammed her orange blossoms to the feet of her surprised would-be bridegroom, marched alone back up the aisle, and swept with gusto out of the church. The stunned guests just sat there in electric silence. Andrew Jackson Brumfield stood rooted to the spot afraid to move—two of Lena Sue's cousins were ushers, and they were linemen on the football team at State. At least the maid of honor, Lena Sue's Yankee roommate from college, and certainly not one of The Twelve, had the grace to faint dead away and fell to the floor. Uncle Ross, the only person who knew what Lena Sue was going to do, with great dignity stepped over her dyed-to-match body and announced, "The reception will be held at the country club as scheduled. I think we could all use some refreshment."

People talked about *that* for years. Yes, The Old Draper House had a rich history.

Claudia and I had thought that Yankee girl Josephine bore watching right from the very beginning. After Lena Sue had decided who had made the cut as bridesmaids when Josephine had accompanied her home one weekend, Lena Sue then started deciding who would have the honor of serving at the reception. She went over who of The Twelve were left and any straggling cousins who would be offended if they were not pouring punch or coffee, or handing out wedding cake.

"An *honor* to serve!" sniffed Josephine as she puffed on a weed. "In Boston we have *servants* to do that!"

We knew right then and there that here was somebody who not only did not know how to do—she was just plain *tacky*.

Hally

AFTER HALLY JORDAN and I had stood in the Almost Wedding of the Century, II, and in lieu of the bride graciously received the guests at the country club reception, Hally went up north to get her master's degree in drama with a scholarship she had won.

I don't remember meeting Hally—I just always knew her. Forever. As toddlers we had attended Sunday School together. Hally had also been in Miss Maude's kindergarten, and she and I were in the same room at school our first six years during which every school day was commenced with the Pledge to the Flag and the Lord's Prayer. In the first grade we both sat at the Tulip table (Claudia and Terry were Roses and Teebo Vincent, a Buttercup). She is the only person I have ever known who made her r's that way—you know, like a stem bearing two leaves. Everyone else made a bridge. Everyone. She, too, was in the brimming car that day, and I spent more time with her than most of The Twelve. Hally and I were members of the same church, and while my mother and her father (first a deacon and then an elder) took year-about being choir director, my mother and her mother, who was a LeFleur, took turns being Chairman of the Women of the Church. This put us in Sunday School together and at church, the youth fellowship and related activities, and the high school band. One of Hally's most distinctive traits was determination. She applied herself to her studies and made the Honor Society our junior year. She tried out for majorette three times before she got a line behind her, but the year I got head majorette, she made drum major and led the whole band. On top of that she got a superior in the state twirling competition, and before she was through she had achieved the highest honor in band—membership in the Lions All-State Band. When she took dancing lessons, her teacher Tess Cochran (Betty Mae's mama) told her mother Emily that Hally had no talent and was always late, and she kicked the child out of class—so when we were sophomores Hally entered the school talent show with a dance she made up herself and won first place over Betty Mae. Hally was in the Miss Addison contest twice before she won that, too. She'd just never give up on anything. In Addison hand-me-downs were a way of life among the little children. It had nothing to do with a daddy's financial status, it was just what was done. Hally was always the tallest girl in our class and when she outgrew her clothes they were always given to me (I passed mine—to include Hally's—down to Bonnie Sullivan). Hally always had lovely things to wear, as her father was the local chiropractor, and I was always delighted to fall heir to her finery. The main thing about Hally was she was particularly kind to everyone, visiting shut-ins and regularly bringing home stray dogs and cats. I think I remember that kindness above all else about her. That, and that after we little girls who played movie star started growing up and not playing movie star anymore, Hally still said she was going to Hollywood. And I didn't doubt that for one minute.

The LeFleurs owned a farm outside of town across the Tallahatchie River, past what was Old Addison. Their family had been among the original settlers in the area, and Miz Blanche, Hally's grandmother, lived alone in the sprawling house out on the farm. Surrounding the home were neat, smaller dwellings inhabited by her farm workers. They tended the land and took care of their beloved Miz Blanche, and she took care of them. From the time I was seven or eight, a special treat was spending a Friday night "out on the place" with Hally at her grandmother's. As the years went by, Hally became kind of the Pallet Party Queen, and at least once a summer, Miz Blanche would actually have The Twelve out to spend the night. Teebo and some of the other boys would come out for a while. We would have a colossal weenie roast, building a big fire on the gravel at the end of the driveway and have hot dogs, corn on the cob from Miz Blanche's garden, baked beans, potato salad, and peach fritters. When we were through roasting the weenies on the coathangers, we would shove marshmellows on them and roast the marshmellows while we sat around the fire and sang "Ninety-nine Barrels of Beer on the Wall" or just joked around. Dex, being the new guy, was frequently the butt of a lot of teasing. Especially about the snipe hunt. When he had first come to Addison a bunch of us invited him to go snipe hunting, and he went for it. Totally. Someone always brought up the snipe hunt.

We had told Dex it was snipe season and how excited we all were about it. That the little varmints had to be caught at night, because the only way to see them was to shine a light in their eyes. This went on for about a month and by the time we got through, Dex was dying to go snipe hunting. He never asked why snipes were so highly prized or even what they looked like.

"We gotta make hay while the sun shines," Terry embellished, "'cause the season is real short this year. Too many people got snipes last year and the population has become endangered." Dex thought it was really nice of us to plan a snipe hunt in his honor. He had been in town for only a few weeks.

One night as it got dark we all gathered in front of Claudia's house. Before we left there, Jimmie Gayle had thought up some pretense for Dex to drive the Trambeau Motors truck so he would have the keys with him. When we had gotten about six cars and trucks full, we all piled in and headed out the Dam Road. "The dam is the best place to catch snipes."

So Travis Dexter was off on his first snipe hunt!

When we got to the dam, we divided into pairs and spread out from the picnic area. Jimmie Gayle the Slick was paired with Dex, and it took only a few minutes before Jimmie Gayle had sneaked off toward the spillway and Dex, desperately trying to find a snipe, had not noticed his departure. We had advised Dex that although the imaginary quarry mainly lived in the woods, there were a lot of them around the picnic area at the dam where they could easily find food—we wanted him to stay in a safe area when he was left alone. We even taught him the snipe mating call and for a while as we distanced ourselves from Dex, we could hear his response to the weirdest sound Teebo had ever made, mimicked by the rest of us as best we could. It sounded like a combination of Alvin the Chipmunk, Tarzan the Ape Man, and a very sick oinking pig.

After we had doubled back to the blow hole in the levee, we piled into all our vehicles except the one left for Dex and beat it back to town and Shug's. About two hours later Dex drove up and moseyed into Shug's looking sheepish indeed.

"Dex! Where you *been*!" we greeted. "Didja get any snipes?"

A crooked grin crept across the face of Travis Dexter. He knew he had been had.

"We got our quota of snipes and jus' couldn't find you *anywhere*!" Terry reported. "We had to get back with our catch before Sher'f Brimley came along."

"Well, I got to feeling rejected when I was out there trying like heck to sound like a really good-looking hunk of a snipe and attract a pretty female snipe and nothing responded but a big ol' bullfrog," Dex responded.

We all burst out laughing and his white teeth appeared in the biggest grin we had ever seen. Dex was a real sport. We all laughed and slapped him on the back, and from that night on he was one of us, included in everything we did, not because he was Jimmie Gayle's cousin, but for himself.

But he would never live down the snipe hunt and someone always brought it up. We shuddered to think what he would do to get us back, but our guard was up.

Before the nights at Miz Blanche's were over, she would have some of her best watermelons iced down and serve them to us out at her picnic table. Miz Blanche's ice cold watermelons were magnificent, and when folks went in to get their groceries from Junior Sullivan, while they were choosing watermelons Miz Blanche's sold out first. When we were almost finished eating the watermelons, it was a ritual to have a watermelon-seed-spitting contest. Everyone had to participate. A contestant would step up to the line gouged in the gravel with a heel and scrooch up his mouth and lips, inhale mightily, and heave/blow the seed as far as possible. Claudia always gave Jimmie Gayle and Terry a run for their money.

Hally had to promise Miz Blanche that the guys would be gone by midnight, and they always were so they would not be banned from the farm during the next pallet party. The next morning Miz Blanche would have a huge breakfast for The Twelve, which included ham and eggs, grits, peaches and strawberries, biscuits and "soggum m'lasses" (sorghum molasses)—all produced on her farm. The only thing we consumed that did not come from the LeFleur place was the coffee.

Knowing Hally and her family background left the town totally unprepared when it got out that she had appeared in the original cast of one of the first Broadway shows depicting total nudity. The family had managed to keep this scoop from the town populace throughout the run—even from Patsy Kay, but when the show was made into a movie featuring the aforementioned original Broadway cast, the jig was up.

When the movie was booked to play at the local picture show, as it was reported to me, "The crowd line to the ticket window snaked two blocks past Draper's Department Store and then turned down the railroad tracks clear past the depot!" The very same depot that had to be rebuilt when the Yankees burned the town to the ground in 1863. Sure enough, there was Hally, "naked as a jaybird" (according to Patsy Kay), dancing and cavorting around the stage along with the man she "lived with without benefit of marriage" (according to Miss Whitley, who would not have been caught dead at the movie but who freely gave reviews of it to any captive audience she could commandeer). This package of unmarried cohabitation and performance in the nude was too much for the little hamlet still asleep in the '60's to accept without comment, and the deafening gossip sent Dr. and Mrs. Jordan on a sudden vacation of undetermined duration.

George, Hally's companion, was offered the pilot of a tv show to be filmed in Hollywood. Hally moved to California with George, whose soon-to-be Top Ten show was to be taped there, and when they made a swing through Addison on their way out to the west coast, the small number of Hally's friends that they saw were quite taken with how nice George was. "Not a movie-star type at all"—not that anyone in Addison had ever met one since our encounter with Robert Mitchum. Dr. and Mrs. Jordan could not believe they liked George so much and hoped to heaven they would just get married.

Hally began teaching acting in Hollywood, and George became famous when his new sit com became the Number One show on televisions across the nation. Eventually an actor, who had made a big initial splash and then dropped out for a few years, made his comeback by winning an Academy Award, and he gave Hally, his acting teacher, full credit right there when he got his Oscar. I recalled how nice Robert Mitchum had been to us. Hally's first movie star. I thought his kindness might have played a role in encouraging her as she steadfastly kept on her path to this success. How different things might have been had he not been so gracious.

Hally got into the New Age goings on, was into healing by crystals, and was yet again the topic of hushed conversations when it got around town that she would not have surgery for her tumor, but was "having needles stuck in all over her" and eating health foods. The early morning coffee crowd at Brown's Cafe got some big laughs out of the jokes big three-hundred-pound Tiny Turnbull made up, but they quit laughing when Hally's tumor disappeared and she had yet to be treated by a doctor.

During a class reunion, one of several I refused to attend, Hally called from Addison to ask me to reconsider, a very sweet gesture and typical of the girl I remembered. John August, who had never participated in any extra-curricular activities and had seldom had anything to do with other students, had decided to put on the whole thing, pay all expenses, and was having the grand finale at his new house out on the highway. He had even gone to Memphis and bought two jukeboxes loaded with nothing but rock-n-roll from the '50's for the sock hop. Hally said she especially had wanted to see me, but I just could not bring myself to go up there—although I desperately wanted to see Hally, most of the people I considered old friends were those I had met in college.

Hally was very understanding and vowed to keep in touch from California, which she did. She continued to call and sent me literature about spirit guides and tapes made by her channeler. I was happy she wanted to preserve our friendship—and glad I had not relented when Hally again called during the reunion weekend and closed with, "I have to go now—Betty Mae is fixing to pick me up. She's carrying me to this afternoon's party"—I knew Betty Mae would be picking me up, too. I hadn't liked her in high school and after Betty Mae came to New Orleans and at Johnnie Kat's suggestion called me for a free room and lunch which she expected me to pay for, I saw no reason to like her now.

* * *

I did, however, witness many memorable events at Betty Mae's house while we were growing up. After youth fellowship on Sunday nights a bunch of the town's teenagers (no Baptists since they held forth until at least ten o'clock) would meet at the telephone booth. It was on the side of the town square and after there were about 15 pairs of headlights shining on it, Teebo Vincent (who would have the family Ford he described as "a sick-lookin' green with a puny yellow streak") or Jimmie Gayle Trambeau would lay down rubber and lead the procession at about 70 miles an hour out to the Dam Road and on to the reservoir. The parade would ride up over the 400-foot spillway to the top of the levee, which was over 100 feet high, and, when Teebo (or Jimmie Gayle) snapped off his headlights, the other 14 pairs were switched off on cue and the cars flew at 90 miles an hour in the darkness clear across the three-mile-long dam. This hot pursuit occurred just about every Sunday night, the moon's being our only light—if indeed it was not obscured by clouds. It is a thousand wonders our dead bodies were not fished out of the Tallahatchie River any given Monday morning. The only teenagers left in Addison would have been Baptists. After arriving back at the city limits, Teebo would usually lead us over to Betty Mae's house which had a big screened-in back porch, and to the horror of Brother Fox Et Al at the Enlightened Morning Star Baptist Church, we would play 45's from Betty Mae's massive collection of records and dance—mostly to Elvis and Fats Domino and The Platters and The Four Lads. This, despite the *New York Times* health warning.

It was there Dan Crockett, who had just moved to town from Texas and was therefore the most popular boy in school, brought *Peyton Place* and read aloud while and Tess and Greezy watched television in the living room and Teebo kept watch. We were even more impressed when we realized Dan had some of the pages actually memorized. I knew a couple of people who had sneaked in and bought copies of the most explosive, sexually-explicit book to rock the decade of the 1950's while they were spending the day in Memphis—and upon returning to Addison kept their smuggled contraband way up under their mattresses with their other paperbacks, away from the eyes of prying parents. Back then everyone knew nothing was ever published in paperback but filthy smut, and one just did not *dare* be seen with any kind of book but a hardbound. But there was Dan Crockett just reading away in public and reciting like crazy. And it was Sunday, too.

Little did we know that this was just a preamble to what was to come. He became known years later for other readings on Sundays, other recitations. He was a widely-known evangelist over in the Delta with record numbers of conversions after each revival. But those Sunday nights on Betty Mae's back porch, we knew we were just plain *evil*!

Brenda Calhoun was a year younger than The Twelve. She was a member of The Enlightened Morning Star Baptist Church. She made straight A's. That would have been admirable if she had not rubbed everybody else's nose in it. She went about it like a cut-throat competitor—as if there were only one A to be had and she would kill to get it. And under any circumstances, Brenda didn't want anybody else making one. It was a badge of honor to her that she went straight home from school every single day and studied. She not only did not dance (I do not know if she read the *New York Times*), but she also did not play cards. Any time she could squeeze in a tacky remark about someone's being in the band or going out for sports, she could be counted on to make it.

I made A's, too, but I took them in stride. So did Hally and Sallybeth. So did every other "A" student we knew. We just made them, and when we had to study for them, we did. Granted, I would have been embarrassed if I had not made A's, but I was willing to work for them when necessary. When anyone asked for assistance with a subject, we gave it. We helped our friends study for tests. I have no idea how many papers I typed far into the night, editing as I went, for Jimmie Gayle and Teebo and Goodness Knows Who Else. Quite frankly, I was flattered to be asked to help. Since we were a grade ahead of Brenda, this "A" business with her was not an issue until we were sophomores and had to share some classes with her. Our junior year the line was drawn in the sand, otherwise known as the threshold to the door of chemistry class.

Sallybeth and I were taking college prep courses, and unfortunately chemistry was on the list. Sallybeth and I decided to be partners in lab and were mortified the day our experiment blew up. Teebo and Jimmie Gayle were in our class, and they joyfully blew things up on a routine basis. Brenda never blew up anything. She just looked disgusted whenever anyone else did and made some snide remark about it, us, or both. She bragged any time her A was higher than ours and made sure no one knew her numerical grade when it was not—never realizing that alone was the tell-tale sign.

It was bad enough *before* the Who's Who contest. Then Brenda, Sallybeth, and I were all finalists for "Most Intellectual Girl." Teebo asked if Sallybeth and I wanted bodyguards. Dex inquired about our life insurance. I was blowing my A's off the scale in every class but chemistry, where I was not even within range, and though Sallybeth was hanging on to her A, Brenda was broadcasting her own 98's and 100's.

Election day dawned. Sallybeth and I both wanted the honor, but the last thing we would have done was campaign. Brenda must have gotten to school at sunup—she was graciously receiving on the front steps by 7:30. Claudia blew one of her graceful smoke rings and said, "I'm surprised she's not giving out orange juice and doughnuts!" When the chorus under the tutelage of my mother met for its morning practice, voting had just taken place and the kids were all abuzz projecting the results. My mother said I probably would not win in view of Brenda. And then, as she reported to me later, there was an outcry of utter dismay—"But *Margie* helps everybody with their homework."

The votes were being counted in study hall. When the classes changed, the librarian would select four or five from the new batch of students and the counting would continue. This went on until all the tallies were made. The results were posted on the bulletin boards in the hall and in the library at the end of the day.

The band was practicing at the football field for our half-time show for Friday night. Teebo's car screeched around the curve by Mrs. Tribble's house. He parked hurriedly and started loping across the grass to the stadium. He waited until we had finished our run-through and called to Sallybeth and me.

"I got the results of the Who's Who contest," he said brandishing a piece of paper. "No one can get more than two titles this year, you know." We knew. "Sallybeth, you're going to have to choose between 'Miss Addison High School,' 'Most Popular Girl,' 'Favorite,' and 'Girl I'd Like to be Marooned on a Tropical Island With'."

"Oh, Teebo, who cares!" Sallybeth cried. "Who got 'Most Intellectual'?"

"Oh, that," Teebo looked downcast. "Well, Sallybeth, you don't get to choose from that."

Sallybeth and I were silent.

Teebo continued, "Margie got *that* all by herself!"

Sallybeth squealed and grabbed me and danced around hugging me.

Teebo slapped me gently on the back and said, "Well done, thy good and faithful servant!" Teebo could not stand Brenda either, and he had *really* had his fill after his last explosion. He figured it was well and good if he blew something up and the *teacher* wanted to speak to that, but it was none of Brenda's business. Besides, Teebo and Jimmie Gayle had come to take a sort of personal pride in their expertise at demolition.

I began to reap congratulations as Sallybeth proceeded to spread the news around the band that I had triumphed over Brenda. I really had not quite realized how deeply the resentment of Brenda ran and how universal it was. Obviously she dealt the same sarcastic remarks and braggadocio to everyone.

I was delighted with my honor and tried to be gracious. The next day when we had chemistry, Miss Addison High School/Most Popular Girl and I strolled into class as usual. Mr. Bernard gave each group a beaker of an unknown concoction and then took us to the lab for us to determine the contents. Sallybeth and I decided we would make a special effort not to have our unknown explode. Teebo and Jimmie Gayle never made decisions of this nature.

Sallybeth and I tried valiantly but could not determine what our mixture was. We labored. We guessed. We fizzled.

Brenda had been the first one to find her unknown. She had been given a beaker of *water*. Sallybeth and I thought the least Mr. Bernard could have done was give her something challenging. Make her sweat for it. Brenda had to come all the way around the room to priss by us before she left the lab, but she did and prissed all the way into the classroom. She was prissing so hard that the thousand petticoats under her pink skirt with the black poodle on it made her skirt hit every lab table right at the poodle's head until she got out of the room. Teebo ambled over and observed, "She ought to be arrested for cruelty to animals."

Slowly the others in the lab found their unknowns. Sallybeth and I continued to struggle. Finally I called to Mr. Bernard. He came back to our station.

"Mr. Bernard, this is potassium chlorate," I announced. "I'm sure it is, but I can't prove it. That's my answer. I speak independently of Sallybeth." If I indeed were wrong, I certainly did not want to be the cause of Sallybeth's losing her A, particularly in the face of Glaring Brenda.

Sallybeth assured Mr. Bernard she stood behind me 100%. Mr. Bernard looked at us thoughtfully and picked up the beaker containing our unknown. "I'll be right back. Y'all go on into the classroom."

Teebo and Jimmie Gayle continued in earnest, but they had been strangely quiet. They usually joked and carried on all during lab. For some unknown reason they were taking this endeavor seriously.

Sallybeth and I went to take our seats when Brenda started.

"I *know* you don't know what you're unknown is." Then glaring at me, "And *you* got 'Most Intellectual Girl'!"

"She certainly did," chimed in Sallybeth. "By the way, Brenda, I noticed you weren't even *nominated* for '*Friendliest*'!" Brenda glared at Sallybeth and turned around to put her nose in her book. I saw Teebo standing in the lab doorway and disappear.

Mr. Bernard came into the classroom and walked to his desk at the front.

"Sallybeth, Margie—I have to apologize to you. You were given some dead chemicals. You could be in there ten years and they'd never react to anything. You are to be commended for coming up with the right unknown. You both get an A." He smiled and said, "I'll be right back—I need to get something from the storage locker for my demonstration." He departed for the storage locker which was outside off the main hall.

I was flabbergasted! Sallybeth's mouth dropped open. The kids around us who had heard Brenda started to giggle.

Then Teebo and Jimmie Gayle rushed in. Jimmie Gayle had a beaker in his outstretched hand. "Mr. Bernard! Mr. Bernard!" Teebo called out excitedly as he came running up the aisle by Brenda's row. This seemed strange since it was obvious Mr. Bernard was nowhere to be seen.

"Mr. Bernard!" called Jimmie Gayle as he dashed up the other side of the row. Just when they got to Brenda, Teebo held out his hand and grabbed the beaker, "Give me that!" he hollered.

"No!" yelled Jimmie Gayle, pulling his hand back.

They tussled a split second before the beaker slipped and broke on Brenda's desk, spreading the vile-smelling sulfuric acid all over her desk and her acres of pink skirt. She jumped up in horror as our classmates scattered all over the room—anywhere the foul-odored Brenda was not. She screamed and shrieked and bellowed at Jimmie Gayle and Teebo, who were as meek as monks and apologizing to kingdom come.

"Don't' tell *me* you're sorry!" Brenda hollered. "You did this on purpose!"

"No, really, Brenda," Teebo stammered with all sincerity, "it was an *accident!*"

"Yeah, an accident—" repeated the eloquent Jimmie Gayle Trambeau as he held his nose, "an accident."

By this time no one could hold in hysterics any longer—the class had not experienced booming chemicals for days, but now it exploded with laughter as Brenda galloped frantically around the room trying to escape her own foul scent and kill Teebo and Jimmy Gayle, not necessarily in that order.

Trey, his timing honed by years on the football field, took his cue and hopped forward to open the door to the hallway just as Brenda rounded Hally's desk up front. Brenda saw the door a straight shot before her and zoomed out into the hall.

Teebo was doubled over chortling. Jimmie Gayle, collapsed in laughter, was sliding down the wall, tears streaming down his face as he tried to catch his breath.

Mr. Bernard re-appeared, still looking out in the hall. "What happened to Brenda?" he asked.

Trey looked thoughtful, "She didn't get 'Most Intellectual Girl'—but she's a shoo-in for 'Miss Aromatic'!" He was laughing so hard he was crying.

Trey could really get going when he got tickled. Like when he told us about Patsy Kay's brother Bubby Lee. One Sunday Trey and Bubby Lee were sitting in the balcony of the Original Morning Star Baptist Church as Brother Fox droned on. They were sitting by a couple of windows in the back, not stained glass but obscure openings not usually noticed. Their glazed, bored eyes kept wandering to the beautiful sunny day that the Lord had provided outside. The trees were green and lush—the magnificent magnolias in Miss Melvina's yard next door were in full bloom, and fuchsia azaleas were ablaze up and down the street. They saw Miss Melvina rocking on the ample front porch of her house, sipping lemonade as she did the warm Sunday mornings that her arthritis prevented her from attending the Methodist Church in the next block.

As the congregation down below fanned themselves—not to keep themselves cool but awake—Bubby Lee was fidgeting and squirming and making all kinds of noises, driving Trey to distraction. Trey was not especially interested in the services being conducted either, but he was ready to throw Bubby Lee over the balcony to the congregation below. A hymn was mercifully announced.

As the voices raised in joyful praise reached a crescendo, Trey leaned over and said to Bubby Lee, "I bet you a dollar you won't jump out the window!"

Although Bubby Lee's daddy owned half the county, this was not reflected in Bubby Lee's weekly allowance, and knowing a good deal when he heard one, Bubby Lee immediately jumped up, raised the window, and made the two-and-a half-story leap to ground below. The stunned Trey was horrified. He knew Bubby Lee was a brick short of a load, but he had not really thought his dare through. Of course Bubby Lee would jump—he had no sense whatsoever. Trey jumped up and leaned out the window just in time to see Bubby Lee scamper around the corner to the front of the church and Miss Melvina faint away.

Trey could not believe that Bubby Lee had not broken both legs and was relieved that he did not. It would not do for Hortense and Sonny not to see Bubby Lee exit the church as they socialized with the congregation after the services. The song the congregation was singing was unexpectedly followed by the recessional, and as Bubby Lee ran up the church's front steps, to his dismay, he saw Brother Fox assuming his place to greet his flock as they exited. For once in his life, Bubby Lee's stupidity gave way to Devine intervention and he raced up to assist as Brother Fox adjusted his robe. Brother Fox got turned around in this procedure and thought Bubby Lee had appeared from inside. He thanked Bubby Lee for his assistance, to which Bubby Lee responded, "Oh, it was nothing—glad to he'p" and graciously extended his hand to the exiting churchgoers who had just been blessed by Brother Fox. "Thank you for coming, Miz Jackson," Bubby Lee said graciously, "—and how's Mr. Jackson doin' since his operation?" This he kept up at the bewildered Brother Fox's side until he saw the amazed Trey Justice—to whom he extended his hand and demanded his dollar.

"We gotta check on Miss Melvina! She saw the whole thing and passed out!" Trey managed to get out urgently despite the laughter he was trying to stifle. He grabbed Bubby Lee from his position of hospitality at the side of Brother Fox and dragged him by his collar down the steps of the church. Hortense waved at them as she caught their eyes, but Trey had Bubby Lee in his clutches and raced them to Miss Melvina's aid. Trey was one of the fastest human beings in the state so they were flying. As they rounded the corner, they screeched to a halt as Trey saw Miss Melvina's daughter at her side. She had propped up Miss Melvina and was administering smelling salts while fanning her mightily.

Trey gave Bubby Lee the dollar and could never understand why Bubby Lee had not at least broken an ankle. He was not even limping. His timing had been perfect, arriving at the church entrance as he did. And there he stood greeting the congregation as if he had preached the sermon himself. Telling about it, Trey mused, "I know Elvis said, 'fools rush in where wise men fear to tread,' but I didn't really think that fool Bubby Lee would jump out a second-story window." Trey could hardly talk—he was just laughing all over himself. "Thankfully Bubby Lee must have landed on his head. No harm done!"

Ted Guy Bledsoe ran the cafe connected with the bus station. When the guys got together late at night, long after the girls were all at home (or at one of Hally's pallet parties), they would congregate there for hamburgers and milk shakes. Ted Guy was very territorial about everything, and certainly did not give service with a smile. One night there was some sort of ruckus in one of the neighboring towns which got blamed on the boys in Addison, who had not even been there. The sheriff, the notorious Toad Watts, came to Addison to investigate and went by Ted Guy's to see if he knew anything about it. Ted Guy was just delighted that Addison teenagers might be in trouble and wanted to do everything possible to cooperate. He started yelling so all the would-be bus passengers and other customers could hear about how all the teenagers in town should be locked up. Ted Guy seemed to overlook the fact that the teenagers were responsible for a large part of his business.

About that time Teebo and Trey drove up, as did Jimmie Gayle and Dex.

Pointing to Jimmie Gayle and Dex, Ted Guy advised, "There's a couple of criminals for you right there."

The Sheriff tore out of the cafe and confronted Jimmie Gayle as soon as he got out of the car. Toad started trying to manhandle him, whereupon Dex strutted forth to intercede. Toad let go Jimmie Gayle's collar.

"You delinquents think you can come over to my town and cause trouble, you gotta 'nother think comin'. I run my town like a law-abidin' community, and we won't have no outside agitators comin' over an' havin' a rumble with our folks." The sheriff started in grabbing Dex, at which point the flash went off from Teebo's trusty Brownie Hawkeye.

The startled sheriff froze and then made a bee line for Teebo with threats of arrest.

"'Scuse me, Sir," began the ever-respectful Teebo, who thought it the wise thing to stay seated in his car, "but aren't you a little out of your jurisdiction?" Trey was unfolding his tall frame out of the door on the other side just in case.

The sheriff apparently either had not thought of that or thought Teebo would not. He was taken aback and started sputtering about the long arm of the law as Ted Guy came lumbering out with "Need some he'p, Sher'f?"

"This ruffian thinks I don't have no 'thority here."

Ted Guy saw it was Teebo and getting close to the sheriff, cautioned out of the side of his mouth so he thought the guys couldn't hear, "Careful—that's Duck Vincent's kid. Even Sheriff Brimley stays hands off. The other one is Trey Justice." Every man in the state knew the name of Trey Justice—not gonna pick a fight *there*!

As Teebo told it, "Suddenly the face of The Toad went 'Oops!' and he couldn't think of any way to get out of this conversation with a power play, so he just kept hollering about what immoral youngsters we were and he was glad he didn't have that kind of trash in *his* county, and Ted Guy invited him to go back inside, but the Sheriff allowed he'd better get back home or his wife would be worried."

The Toad scratched off a la Biff Johnson as Ted Guy went back inside.

"You know Ted Guy put him on us," said Dex. "He's always trying to give us trouble."

"Aw, he can't do anything," Teebo said. "Let's go in and have a couple o' aggravating burgers."

The quartet ambled inside and slid into their customary last booth over by the far window. Ted Guy hated that they never sat at the counter where he could antagonize them and he had to take all that energy to go clear over yonder to the booth to take their order. They were much more easily harassed at the counter.

If Jack Nicholson thought he gave the waitress a hard time in "Five Easy Pieces," he should have witnessed the order-taking any given night at the bus station. The boys got Ted Guy so confused that he finally just said,

"Four hamburgers with everything. Take off what you don't want yourself." He slammed the order into the window to the kitchen and the boys plotted their next move.

"It's time we got Ted Guy for all the grief. This goes on all the time," Jimmy Gayle said.

"Yeah, I wouldn't mind so much, but all this mess on top of all the short changing he does. I'm getting ticked," Teebo replied. "If you don't give him the exact amount you owe, he doesn't bring any change. If you give him a big bill, he'll give you back something, but not what's due. When Terry said something about it, he said it was policy to add an automatic tip to the check."

"Yeah," said Jimmie Gayle, "and for non-existent service. Trouble is, this is the only place we have to go this late."

Some of the other boys began arriving—Terry, Dan Crockett, and a few others. When the burgers were ready, Ted Guy delivered them to the table by slamming them down so hard the plastic plates rolled around upon impact.

The boys returned knowing glances. Teebo rose from the booth and went out to his car. He rummaged around in the back seat as Ted Guy eyed him like a hawk, as if hoping he would drive off without paying so Sheriff Brimley could be called. Teebo reappeared in the cafe momentarily, picked up the red bottle, and began slinging ketchup on his burger.

Jimmie Gayle then slid off the seat and went outside. Again Ted Guy ran to the door to watch him. Jimmie Gayle came back inside and resumed eating. Teebo then repeated his trip outside to his car and back. He stopped by Dan, whispered something, and then, smiling at Ted Guy, said, "Ted Guy, I didn't get a drinka water. Would you please bring me a drinka water?" and went back to the job of devouring his hamburger. The guys snickered at Teebo's famous drink of water, and it was Dex who went next. Jimmie Gayle hopped up to let him out of the booth, and Dex went out the door. Ted Guy was getting curious. Dex returned. He whispered to Terry and came back to the table. Teebo went outside yet a third time just as two schoolbuses full of band members from down state stopped with about sixty hungry, thirsty, screaming kids. They stormed the diner like the beach at Normandy. The pinball machines started ringing. Ding! Ding! Ding! Ted Guy went into shock. He was the only person to wait on the standing-room-only crowd. The children were yelling at each other back and forth across the diner and shouting at Ted Guy. "Four hamburgers and three orders of fries!" "A cheeseburger and a coke!" "I want a milkshake!"

"Where's the bathroom?" Ted Guy could not hear to take the orders. Ding! Ding! Ding! There was only one cook in the back. No local residents felt particularly obligated to assist Ted Guy in this, his moment of need, so they did not offer their help with the customers and sat back to enjoy the show. They continued to go in and out of the cafe and return to the badly-needed booth. In fact, they were taking a sort of sadistic pleasure in Ted Guy's frantic discomfort. What few orders Ted Guy could write down were utterly confused, the cook kept asking what he had written, Ted Guy couldn't read it either, and the whole place was a disaster. The band kids kept screaming and complaining, along with the chaperones. Ding! Ding! Ding! "I couldn't find the bathroom!" "Where's my chicken salad sandwich?" Then two Trailways buses appeared and disgorged their full complements of passengers.

More people. More orders. More dinging. More shouting. More complaints. Teebo ambled up to the counter and gently inquired, "I beg your pardon, Ted Guy, I didn't get my drinka water? Remember I needed a drinka water?" He coughed.

Ted Guy blew up. "Get outta here! G'wone. Git!"

Innocently Teebo asked, "What did we do? I just wanted my drinka water. I'm supposed to get a glass when I sit down. And I ordered a *meal*! We were here before these—these—*tourists*!"

Jimmie Gayle was almost sliding under the table with laughter.

"Git!" boomed Ted Guy.

Trey slid out of the booth and stood very tall beside Teebo in front of Ted Guy and peered directly down into his face.

Ted Guy cowered and muttered, "I've got to see to my customers."

The four slowly sauntered through the bedlam toward the door.

"Git!" fumed Ted Guy from behind the covered pineapple upsidedown cake.

"All I wanted was a drinka water," Teebo said sadly as he passed him.

All of the local boys left Ted Guy in the cauldron of swarming band members, who were throwing spit balls, potato chips, bellowing for service, and snatching ash trays and ketchup bottles amid the Trailways passengers.

Since Ted Guy had thrown out the Gang of Four Et Al, they had not had the opportunity to pay. For weeks after that when Ted Guy would refill the napkin holders he would find a customer check for a hamburger and a coke or milkshake—with or without potato chips—and wonder where on earth it had come from and cuss with disgust that despite his eagle eye, yet someone else had left the cafe without paying and wanted to make sure Ted Guy knew about it.

One Sunday night after our obligatory flirt with death on the levee at the reservoir, we came back to town and Teebo, in the lead, headed out on the highway. He turned off on a gravel road and drove several miles to the south. I was in the car with Jimmie Gayle.

"Does anybody know where we're going?" I asked.

"I think he's going to that old church," Trey replied. "He and I heard about it and drove by last week—it's been abandoned for years—I think it was built before the Civil War."

Civil War. Civil War. Civil War. It seems we were born knowing about the Civil War. We grew up talking about it. We talked about it as though it had happened during World War II instead of almost a hundred years ago. It could have been in our genes—in the pure artisan spring water we drank. The homes and farms of our ancestors had been devastated during the conflict. We had never heard of any plantations in the county—Beau Rivage was over the county line and stories about it were more legend than history as far as we knew. Families worked their small farms as best they could. Our knowledge had to do with their survival. It was part of our lives. We knew where the Yankees had ridden through. We knew they had burned our town to the ground. We knew how Cousin Geralynn had hidden Great-Aunt Gillian's jeweled necklace in the root cellar. We knew where our Great Grandfathers had served and under Whose command. It could have happened last week. Now we could look at medals for bravery during World War II. My friends and I could not remember that either, but we knew in the tradition of their ancestors, the sons of Addison had done their duty, risen to the call and served their country. The United States of America. Devotion to duty. Honor. Protection of family. We had Southern roots, and we were Americans. It never occurred to us that there might be a conflict of interest there. The history of the South was part of the history of the United States. Like the history of settling the West. We were proud Americans living in the greatest country on earth. We revered the military and were proud of the sons of our town who had served in World War II.

"Why are we going out there in the middle of the night?" asked Sarah Jane.

"He just prob'ly wants you girls to get scared, S'erJane," Trey mused.

"Well, he's got another think coming," retorted Hally.

"I don't think Teebo'd try to frighten us," I defended. "He just probably wants to show us what y'all found."

The darkness of the country was relieved only by the moonlight as it shone through the tentacles of the dense trees on both sides whose branches joined over our heads as though they were arms reaching to each other, making dancing patterns of the leaves which raced from the hood of the car to the trunk as we sped in the dust after Teebo. All the country roads were surrounded by thick, beautiful trees and vines or by endless fields of cotton. There was low, flat land as far as the eye could see, and the straight rows of cotton plants stretched in the distance to the point they met the sky. The only change in the landscape was thick woodlands, the occasional house in the middle of the cotton fields, or an expanse of rich, green pasturelands where slowly grazing cows meandered during the day.

Finally Teebo pulled onto a dirt path, and there in the moonlight stood a small, neat little church building with a steeple nestled in the tree tops which caressed it in the gentle breeze of the night.

We spilled out of the cars and trudged up the path. We had long since learned to have flashlights available on these Sunday-night forays, and a couple clicked on. The guys ambled around, and Teebo climbed through a window and then opened the front door. We were hesitant to go in, but none of us stayed outside.

The sanctuary was musty and it was hard to breathe. Some boards were missing from the floor, so we walked very carefully. It was so dusty that coughing and sneezing commenced as we inched our way forward.

"My dress is gonna get dirty," complained Betty Mae.

"Shut up, Betty Mae," someone in the back sighed.

Dex zipped up to the pulpit and began his oratory, "My fellow Christians, brethren and sistren—" Then he saw the organ. By this time Teebo had arrived at the altar, and he and Dex raised the covering over the keyboard.

Teebo sat down and both his hands came down hard on the keys, "You ain't nothin' but a hound dog," he sang, "Cryin' all the time."

"No doubt you're dedicating that to Betty Mae," Dex teased.

"Now, Dex, there was no call for that," pouted Betty Mae.

There was no sound from the organ.

"It's broken," Teebo announced.

"Well, what did you expect?" said Hally. "It's been here since the Civil War."

"Probably 'cause Sherman couldn't *find* this God-forsaken place!" said the nervous Betty Mae. "Let's leave."

"This place isn't God forsaken, Stupid," came a voice from behind. "This is a *church*."

"Well, *somebody* forsook it—who called me 'Stupid'?" Betty Mae wanted to know.

"Wait a minute," Trey said, "it's a *pump* organ." He moved over to the edge of the bench and bent down. He pushed hard. The wood began to creak and hiss. Teebo continued his mock concert as though he were Lon Chaney as the Phantom of the Opera. He swayed and rolled around on the bench and was apparently transfixed with his own non-music. His hands kept going up in flourishes like Liberace's, as Trey kept pushing. Suddenly as Teebo's hand banged down again, a loud roar came from the organ. We all screamed and jumped back. That the organ would make a sound was the last thing we expected—no one could *believe* it! We were thrilled!

Teebo came down on the keys again. Another loud wail. Trey was really pushing hard. "Move over, Teebo," instructed Sallybeth as she slid down on the bench. "Help Trey pump!"

Teebo complied and Sallybeth began playing "Amazing Grace." We all started singing, "Am-aaa-zing Grace, how sweeeeet thuh sound—" A lot of the keys remained silent when struck and the rest were out of tune, but our joyful noise continued to rise to the empty belfry. Sallybeth had a beautiful voice and could harmonize in a very high range. We sounded pretty good!

We continued with "In the Garden"—"An Dee walks with me an Dee talks with me, an Dee tells me I am His own"—and after "Onward, Christian Soldiers" we made sure the cover was securely over the keys and started toward the door.

"I can't *believe* a working organ was left here," I said.

"Maybe the place is haunted," Betty Mae speculated. "Maybe everybody ran out never to return." Betty Mae could be very dramatic.

"Y'all go on out and I'll lock up and go out the window," Teebo volunteered. We heard the lock click behind us and Teebo's steps recede. Jimmie Gayle tried the door to be sure it was secure. We were always careful to leave everything as we had found it, locked up tight. Although no one claimed ownership to most of our targets, we respected the fact the property was not ours. We had been slipping into old vacant houses for years—the furniture in some of them had been undisturbed since the Civil War despite our many exploratory expeditions. Even Claudia never smoked around them, reverently declaring, "This is our *heritage*!"

"This place *must* be haunted," Betty Mae continued. "Look over yonder. There's a cemetery right *there*!" She pointed to a small fence beyond which broken marble pillars reflected brightly in the moonlight.

"Of course it's not haunted," Jimmie Gayle replied. "It's a *church*. Anyway, if it is, we just woke the dead."

"Well, I hope it counts we were singing hymns," Betty Mae replied.

Teebo came around the corner of the church, "Did I hear someone say 'haunted'?"

"It's just Betty Mae," informed Jimmie Gayle. "Don't pay any attention."

"Well, I hear it *is*—let's see if we can see the ghost in the cemetery," Teebo grinned.

"Not me!" Betty Mae was ready to roll.

"I hear there's a headless Civil War soldier that rides his horse through the graveyard on nights just like *this*!" Teebo began. He winked at me.

"No!" Betty Mae was emphatic. "I want to go home!"

"He comes down the road and his horse jumps the fence—"

"Hush, Teebo!" Betty Mae was getting mad. But as we neared the cemetery, I noted she was moving with us, not heading to the cars alone.

Sallybeth started singing softly, "Am-aaa-zing—ing Grace, how sweeeeet thuh sound—"

Teebo continued mysteriously, "The soldier was betrayed by a spy and the Yankees attacked and his girlfriend got killed." Teebo was good.

"There he goes again," I thought. "Just like in class when he gets a drink of water." He was making it up as he went and Betty Mae was buying the whole thing.

"That sa-aavd a wretch li—iike meeeeee—" sang Sallybeth.

"Ooooooooo—" Dex moaned like a ghost.

Hally and I stifled giggles.

"Hush up, Dex!" Betty Mae ordered.

Dex was undeterred, "Oooooooo—oooooooooo—"

We saw there was a well by the gate to the cemetery.

"Oh, I—IIIII wa-uz lost—" continued Sallybeth.

"I wonder if there's any water in there," Jimmie Gayle tapped the cover.

"The soldier was so enraged that the spy caused the death of his beloved, that he swore she would be avenged—" Teebo's voice was a low drawl.

"And now—ow am found," Sallybeth continued.

"Ooooooo—ooooo!"

Jimmie Gayle and Teebo raised the cover on the well and slid it off the side.

Teebo resumed, "The soldier found the spy and shot him." Teebo began to walk directly toward Betty Mae. "The spy got off a shot, mortally wounding the soldier, and he rides on moonlit nights looking for his love."

"Teebo, that's enough!" Betty Mae stomped her foot.

"Was blind an—an—d now I see."

"Oooooo!"

"Shut up, Travis Dexter!"

"I didn't say anything," responded Dex. We had started back to the cars.

"Did, too—I heard you!" Betty Mae shook her finger at Dex.

"No, I *didn't*!" Dex was emphatic.

"Hey, Dex is over *there*!" Teebo exclaimed. "And the sound came from—from the *well*!"

We all pulled up short. Sallybeth's serenade ceased. No one said anything, and we were afraid to move.

"Oooooo—oooooo"—the sound *did* come from the well!!!

Jimmie Gayle looked at Teebo—"What should we do? Shine a light down there?"

"I—I—I don't think so," Teebo advised. "Why don't we just—"

Abruptly a loud, full screech came from the well—there was no mistake!

"I'm going to faint," Betty Mae said weakly.

"Don't you dare!" I commanded. "We'll leave you here—Okay gang, let's *go*!"

"Yeah, everybody," agreed Jimmie Gayle. "Let's boogie!"

Before we could even turn around, the screech started at the bottom of the well and rose in volume and pitch as it continued to rise to the surface. We were frozen in place, our eyes locked on the well.

"Oooooo-OOOOOOOO-**OOOOOOOOO**—" the sound was coming up from the well toward us!

Suddenly enormous flapping, screeching, loudly fluttering wings flew from the well and a loud wail came forth as it rose into the air.

"Oooooooo—ooooo—ooooo!" The wings landed on the graveyard fence and wailed again. We saw they were attached to a huge hoot owl that turned its head and glared at us. Then the figure took to the air and flew silently over the tombstones and into the trees.

We burst into nervous, relieved laughter. All except Betty Mae—she was shrieking bloody murder at the top of her lungs while being chased to the cars by Dex, arms flapping, as he wailed, "Ooooo—oooo—oooooo!"

Betty Mae

BETTY MAE WAS the only adopted child in town. None of us thought anything of it—we had known she was "adopted" before we knew what that meant, and it was just a detail about her like her blond hair. We usually forgot about it. From the time we were at Miss Maude's she had been very bossy, and changed best friends among us about once a week. She was spectacularly indulged by Tess and Greezy—anytime Betty Mae wanted anything, either Tess or Greezy would hit the road for Memphis post haste—Betty Mae rarely wanted anything that could be purchased in Addison. One week when I was Betty Mae's best friend during our stint in the third grade, she and I went over to the funeral home and asked Mr. Dinkins to show us the embalming room. The startled Mr. Dinkins had never before had a request such as this, but no one had died in the past couple of days, so he took us in for a minute or two, gave us a non-informative explanation of what was done there, and ushered us out. I had thought it was very interesting and was ready to go see if Von Graham could fix a banana split for two, but Betty Mae suddenly said she was going home and off she went. I happen to know that to this day she has never attended a funeral.

In high school, dating Betty Mae became sort of a ritual of passage for the guys, since she was known to be fairly easy and they could feel her up just about any old time. After high school graduation she continued to teach dancing at her mother's dancing school and dated whatever men came through every few months to work at the gas company. No one lasted very long, but they knew at this point they could do more than feel her up.

John August was in our high school class and lived out in the country. He was a nice-looking boy, but pretty much kept to himself and maintained a B average. He never mixed with those of us who lived in town and although everyone liked him, that was it. He never went to any of our parties, never showed up on weekends at anything, to include the picture show, and was never at Shug's. At some point he and Betty Mae became friends, as with alphabetical seating he sometimes sat immediately in front of her, but they never dated or anything—didn't even socialize at recess, and since Betty

Mae never mentioned him, his anonymity continued. But that all changed the day that Baxter Bridges disappeared.

After the initial find and flurry of discovery around our freshman year in high school, the interest in Beau Rivage Castle waned and no one paid any attention to it for a couple of years. Then one cold winter day during the holidays John and Baxter Bridges, another country boy in our class, went out hunting nearby and that afternoon realized that a sudden storm was about to break. The day had dawned beautiful and crisp, ideal for hunting. The boys had set out with Baxter's dog Ol' Hawk at daybreak, and they had packed small knapsacks for their lunches. It seemed that a glorious day had in one minute changed to one darkened by black clouds ready to empty the sky on the cotton fields and forests below. The temperature dropped dramatically to a freezing chill. As the rain began, they saw Beau Rivage Castle in the distance and headed toward it for shelter. As the boys and Ol' Hawk neared the ruin, the rain began to pelt them ferociously. They stopped under a tree to see that the storm was getting worse, and the low-lying fields were not draining. The mud was slush, and lightning struck a tree close to Baxter as he tore through what must at one time have been a garden.

Reaching the porch, they carefully made their way through the rotting wood, hoping to find a place near the stone wall on the side to keep them dry and out of the wind. The dog tried to shake off the water soaking in his coat, and Baxter jumped to stay out of the resulting spray.

As the thunder crashed about them, Baxter remarked that he couldn't remember such abrupt, violent weather. The darkness was suddenly complete and with the torrent descending and the nearby creek rising between them and their family farms, they thought they might be there for the rest of the night. Ordinarily they would not have minded camping out, but they had certainly not planned on this turn of events and the cold was going right through them despite their hunting clothes. The dog seemed agitated—quite unlike Ol' Hawk, who obviously loved to go prowling the countryside with his master. He began to dart back and forth, yapping intermittently. He had braved rain, cold—all of the elements—and relished being at the side of Baxter Bridges, Mighty Hunter. This behavior was uncharacteristic of him.

Baxter told John not to bother about Ol' Hawk and hunkered down in a dry corner. The dog would no doubt settle down as soon as he became accustomed to the new place that they had found for themselves. When the guys caught their breaths, they decided to make a fire—there was certainly ample wood scattered around. The challenge would be to find enough that was dry. They were able to gather the wood and some brush which had been blown within the compound long before the rain and easily got a fire going.

They settled back again against the wall, watching the flame grow taller as they listened to the wind howl and rain become more furious. Actually they were quite pleased with themselves—they had put together a snug little oasis here in the storm. They had room to stretch out, they and Ol' Hawk were sheltered from the raging weather, and there were some snacks in their small packs to keep hunger away. They enjoyed each other's company and each was glad not to be alone. Ol' Hawk kept pacing. He seemed to have calmed down somewhat, but periodically he acted as though something were attracting his attention and he would just stand there and growl.

Baxter held out his hand, "Come on over here, Dawg. Get warm by the fire." Ol' Hawk ignored him. "Hawk! Com'ere." Ol' Hawk gave a last bark at the air and turned his attention toward his master. "Here, Hawk," Baxter gestured again. Ol' Hawk obeyed. "Good boy." He ran his hand over the dog's wet coat. "Lemme see—I think I've got a towel in here or somethin'." He dug into his pack, grateful to find a thermos of coffee he had forgotten he had packed, and pulled it out with a towel.

"Yep, we'll get you dry." He wiped his own face first and then set about rubbing the dog gingerly with the towel. The dog stood still for the first time, and his master quickly had him as dry as he could get. Baxter placed the towel to dry on a fallen beam nearby and the dog lay down by the fire.

By this time the fire had become a nice size. They had made it on a portion of the stone floor and had placed a few broken pieces of stone around it to assure it would not spread dangerously. As they leaned against the wall staring into the glow, they felt very peaceful. They were glad they had been close to Beau Rivage Castle when this unexpected storm had hit. It would be adequate for the night if it came to that.

John said, "I wonder how many nights I've camped out. Hundreds. When I was a little boy out on the place, I tromped through the woods near the house, and I've always fished and hunted. My dad taught me how to shoot as soon as I was strong enough to hold a gun, and he took me over the fields and out into the woods on campouts from the time I was six or seven years old. We would lie in the darkness by the fire and listen to the hoot owls and the other sounds of the night, and we'd lie on our backs and Daddy taught me about the stars—the Big Dipper, the Little Dipper."

Baxter said his mama had read him a story when he was little about a ship that sailed without a compass—it had used the North Star, and he had insisted on learning how to use it to get directions. Little Baxter had been secure in the knowledge that if he ever got lost in the jungles of Africa, he could find the North Star and direct himself back to civilization and Addison. His parents never worried that he would get lost.

"My daddy taught me about the constellations and told me stories 'bout Greek mythology—Apollo, Zeus, Pandora and her box—I was ready to go save everybody!" he laughed. "He told me about the planets, and we'd speculate 'bout life on Mars or Venus. I remember when I saw my first shooting star, I thought we'd been invaded by aliens!"

"I remember when I saw mine—I was so excited I couldn't stand it," John said.

Baxter's dad had told him stories around their campfires. Stories of Indians—Cherokee, Black Foot—there were several tribes whose ancestors had trod these very fields—tales of cowboys, and legends of the Civil War. Since the War had affected the ancestors of all but newly-arrived families in the area, stories of relatives were passed through the generations. The escapades of the dashing officer James Tillotson Addison were legendary. There were plenty of stories to tell.

John asked, "Were you in Miss Greenway's class last year when Johnnie Kat told about her ancestor Miss Iris Rose when the Yankees came down?"

"Yeah," replied Baxter. "The Damnyankees swept down through here and burned the town to the ground—the only thing they left standing on the square was the court house." They had taken over the Botty house, and Johnnie Kat Botty had proudly said the bullet holes are still in her grandmother's dining room table. Miss Iris Rose had no warning the Yankees were about to take over her house, and when she saw the soldiers in blue coming up the sidewalk, she made a torch out of living room pillows, but the Yankees got inside before she could burn the place down. It got all over the northern part of the state that she had rather watch her heritage go up in flames than have Yankees sitting comfortably in her home, and when everyone saw the devastation throughout the land that the Yankee soldiers left in their wake, she became a heroine."

A woman prepared to make such a sacrifice to keep them out of her midst did not inspire trust in the Yankees who commandeered her home, so Miss Iris Rose was watched constantly while under house arrest. But she managed to sneak a shotgun and marched in to the dining room one night while the captain was entertaining, fully prepared to give the guests a show they would never forget. She aimed the barrel at the captain's surprised head, but a quick aide knocked the gun down. She managed to get off a shot before they wrestled it away from her. The bullet went clear through the table right into the captain's leg. She was spirited upstairs and locked up, but she managed to do the very same thing two weeks later and shot the captain in the same leg again. There was no telling what would have happened to her (although the captain was more embarrassed that the same infraction had occurred twice than that he was harmed) if some messenger had not rushed in right that very minute with a false report about Confederates riding over toward Oxford, so Miss Iris Rose was spared along with her house and became known as Iris Rose, the Thorn in the Captain's Side.

The boys had continued to exchange the lore of the area, and after a while the fire's hypnotic glow and dancing flames had made them drowsy. They had been up since dawn. They got out the knapsacks for the remnants of their lunches and some candy bars, and Baxter pulled out some treats he always kept in the sack for Ol' Hawk.

"Here, Hawk," he said in the dog's direction and put the treats before him. The dog, staring toward a corner, then turned toward his master and responded with enthusiasm to the food.

Baxter munched on the chocolate and poured some of the coffee from his thermos. It had felt good warming them. This unexpected turn of events had not turned out so badly.

They watched the fire and listened to the wood crackle in the blue and yellow heat. This was probably just like the fires built by the Chickasaw Indians. A brilliant flash of lightning startled them right before a deafening crash of thunder. Ol' Hawk jumped up and began to snarl straight at the fire—a vicious, growling howl quite unlike him.

"It's okay, Hawk—calm down," Baxter had said. He had reached out to the animal to pet him, but by now Ol' Hawk was barking savagely at the flames as though the fire had attacked. Baxter got up and went to the dog, put his arms around him and began to stroke his back in an attempt to calm him.

"Shhhh—it's okay, Hawk. Everything's all right. It's just the storm. We're okay. Calm down." He continued to try to comfort Ol' Hawk, who apparently wanted none of it. Finally, he got the dog to stretch out again and lie down beside him as he continued to run his hand gently down the dog's back.

The boys were against the wall and facing the fire. John had gotten comfortable leaning against the stone. They were both very sleepy and Baxter commented the blaze seemed to cast a spell. They laughed as their eyes grew heavy. The flames danced inside the circle of stones. Just as Baxter said he thought he was having visions of the Chickasaws, the sound of the rain in its fury seemed to take on a steady beat, but a strangely slow, rhythmic one. The beat of drums. Louder and louder. They could not take their eyes from the fire. The drums beat faster. Louder. A small swirl of blue smoke began to rise from the fire. Slowly it rose and expanded. Ol' Hawk jumped up again and began to bark at the fire. The drums beat harder. The circle of smoke grew wider. The boys could hear the rain. The thunder. The drums. The angry bark of the dog. The drums were deafening. The dog's barking was painful to hear.

"Eyes! Looking at us! Do you see them? Right in the fire!" screamed John.

"Y-y-yes—!" Baxter, terrified, squeezed his eyes shut and slammed his hands to his ears. The eyes continued to stare at them and rise from the flames. It was an evil, frightening stare. A face began to form around them and the upper body of a woman. The boys were looking at an Indian maiden emerging from the flames! There was a blinding flash of lightning, a roar of thunder, and then all was quiet. The rain had abruptly stopped. The sudden silence was powerful. Everything was still. Even Ol' Hawk.

John leaped to his feet. "Let's get out of here!" he exclaimed. He slid on the strap to his knapsack as he rose. "Get up, Bax—let's go!" Baxter could not get his breath. John helped him up. "We can't stay here another minute. Storm or not. It's let up now. Let's go before it starts up again!"

Baxter tried very hard to get going, but he stumbled and fell. "I can't—"

"Yes, you can. You've got to. I'll help you," encouraged John. He would not let Baxter give up, and somehow they got away from Beau Rivage Castle and back to the Bridges' place. John was totally exhausted from half carrying Baxter all the way home, slogging through the mires of mud. Both of the boys were covered with ooze and dirt and suffering from the bitter cold when they collapsed on the Bridges' porch. They were still terribly afraid.

They told their story in detail to Baxter's parents, who listened to their unbelievable adventure with concern but who really thought the boys were just delirious from their awful experience in the weather. Mrs. Baxter immediately got Baxter to bed and Mr. Bridges took John home in his pickup.

The boys continued to insist what they had experienced at Beau Rivage Castle was the real thing, that they were not hallucinating, and they had not made it up. They told the same story over and over. They described everything. They reiterated their conversations. Itemized the food they had. Their families kept asking questions. The same answers came from both boys. A deputy even interviewed John despite the fact there was no illegality here. Baxter was too upset to see him. No one doubted the boys believed what they said, but their parents and others thought it was just a result of their trauma.

Baxter continued to be sick in bed the next few days and one morning when his mama woke up and went in to check on him, he was not there. She looked all over the house and the yard. She called to her husband in the barn, who had not seen him. They looked everywhere. The August family did not have a telephone, so Mr. Bridges drove his pickup over to see if Baxter had gone over there despite his weak condition. John was still asleep, but seeing how alarmed Mr. Bridges was, Mrs. August woke him up.

John staggered out of his room trying to wake up and said, "I haven't seen him, but he's at Beau Rivage Castle."

The surprised Mr. Bridges said, "How do you know?"

"I just dreamed it. He's there. I *know* it."

Mr. Bridges responded, "He's sick. He's too weak to possibly get there."

John was emphatic. "*He's there.*"

Mr. Bridges did not agree, but he had no other lead. He rushed to his pickup and drove it as close to Beau Rivage Castle as he could. He ran up to the ruin and found Baxter's red baseball cap on the remnants of the porch. He had seen it the night before on the hat rack by the door at home. He called to Baxter and Ol' Hawk came bounding out barking.

"Where's Bax, Hawk? Where is he, Boy?" he made a motion for Ol' Hawk to show him. Hawk turned and ran to the back wall.

Mr. Bridges found the remains of the fire that the boys had built and the smoldering embers of another almost burned out—but no Baxter. He looked on the other side of the wall and found some footprints in the mud. They led to the Tallahatchie on the other side of the field. Baxter's jacket was on the bank.

The neighboring farmers came to help in the search. Sheriff Brimley was even called in. The town buzzed and volunteers came from all around. They scoured the countryside. They even dragged the river. Baxter Bridges could not be found.

This event called John to our attention more than ever before. When he came back to school, we tried to include him in our fellowship, but he preferred to remain apart. We tried to let him know we would be there for him, but we respected his privacy—whatever had happened must have been horrible and it had certainly taken a classmate from our midst. What we knew in our circle came from town talk and Teebo's reports, which we knew were based on the official investigations and his own reliable research. To her credit, even Patsy Kay did not quiz John about Beau Rivage.

When we graduated from high school, John went to State and worked in the drug store on weekends. So everyone knew what he was doing but did not particularly take any notice. Even Patsy Kay. John got his degree in pharmacy and came back to Addison to fill prescriptions.

The small town was shocked one Thursday when *The Addisonian* came out with Betty Mae's wedding announcement that she would soon marry John August. After all, who *was* that boy? More important, who was his *family?* Although they had of course surfaced during the Baxter Bridges business, that had been the extent of their celebrity. Tess was so distraught she told Betty Mae she would mortgage the house and take her to New York to study dancing if she'd **just not marry John August**. But Betty Mae had made up her mind. Greezy had by now lost the farm and was working at the local hardware store, so Betty Mae became the first of many to borrow Lena Sue Crawford's ill-fated wedding dress. The couple was married in a quiet ceremony out at Mount Olive close to the farm owned by John's parents, and after a honeymoon weekend in Memphis at the Hotel Peabody, John and Betty Mae rented an apartment in the new housing complex. Before long they built a nice little house out on Chelsea Drive.

John eventually opened his own drug store right off the town square. He hired a couple of people to jerk sodas and help out with the cosmetics and the cash register. John appeared to be conducting a successful business when he and Betty Mae soon built a bigger house out on the highway. Then they added some rooms to it. Since no one in particular was ever invited out there, the only source of information was the local contractor's daughter, who would occasionally mention such as this while she played bridge—and of course Tess, but she had been exaggerating about Betty

Mae since the day they had brought her home from the orphanage. Pretty soon the aforementioned contractor's daughter announced that John had extended an offer of employment to Lucy Clanton, who had just graduated from high school. Patsy Kay had said some time before that Lucy had a crush on John, but he was always back in the pharmacy department counting pills, so no one gave it any thought. No more than John had ever received. John was very serious about the business he now owned and felt he must keep tabs on it even when he was at home—so he installed intercoms in the store that he connected to his house. This was no secret, and people around town were very impressed with his innovative technology. But not so impressed as Betty Mae was the day John forgot to turn it off while she sat in her very own bedroom and heard John and Lucy as they copulated right there in the drug store behind the analgesics. Betty Mae hired a lawyer from Clarksdale to sue John for a divorce. John took out the intercom, but that was a mute point by then since Betty Mae had already gotten the house.

John quickly got married again, not to Lucy, but to Frances Grace Dunbar who had just moved to town from Itta Bena. Another big house went up on the highway at the other end of town and one day Frances Grace came home early from Memphis to find John copulating with Lucy in the master bedroom. Martha Louise Potter hurriedly put together a bridge party so that this bit of news could be duly reported, and the ladies there representing the Enlightened Morning Star Baptist Church promised to foray into the subject at the very next prayer meeting. Josey Hanks volunteered to host the next day's bridge game. Not much had been learned over night, so the ladies assembled that afternoon had to just watch Debbie Deaton go down in flames when she bid seven no trump.

One day right after *that* divorce John stopped at Shug's on his way to Memphis, just needing something to tide him over until he got to Leonard's up from Graceland and got some of that barbecue. Tallulah Barnes had just mastered carhopping duties and masterfully hopped into John's car at his impromptu invitation when he casually mentioned he would buy her a new skirt and sweater set at Goldsmith's if she would accompany him to Memphis. After more barbecue at the Rendezvous Room they enjoyed each other immensely at the Hotel Peabody until after breakfast grits the next morning, and the next Saturday John got Elmo Tidmore, Justice of the Peace, a title which belied the havoc this ceremony would cause, to officiate at their nuptials. By now John had the drill down to a science—the new house went up on the highway on the *west* side of town (fortunately the intersections of the two highways so far left room for John to build in another direction).

The contractor had built his own mansion by now in view of John's various domestic upheavals, and his daughter decided to give a housewarming bridge party as soon as it was finished. Everyone was brought up to date, except it was not known if John had gotten Tallulah in trouble. The next day's ladies circle didn't Enlighten the Ladies any more than the bridge party, so John did a land-office business in Coca-Cola and cosmetics sales for the next two weeks.

Time marched on and one day John came home while Robert Sample's tv repair truck was sitting in the driveway. John did not think anything about it, as Robert always had to come install new tv setups when John's new houses were finished. He thought more about it when he found Tallulah on the kitchen table with Robert on top of her without his pants. The couple was too involved to notice John's untimely entrance, so when he went to his car for his gun and sneaked back inside, he was able to take careful, unnoticed aim at Robert's naked butt.

It was a good thing John always built away from town. No one heard the gun shot, and Robert was not in a position to press charges—his wife's being pregnant, for one thing (it also would not do for it to get out that Robert could not be trusted to repair televisions in the various homes in town), so they got him to the doctor's office with some story about a hunting accident. But Tallulah didn't fair too well in the aftermath and the last time Patsy Kay reported on her whereabouts, she was still performing on top of tables, but these were on the Gulf Coast in a strip joint.

I guess all these adventures sort of brought John out. The latest house out on the highway was a great place to have the class reunion. Even with two jukeboxes, no neighbors complained about the noise and everyone had such a good time at all the festivities John planned that they are still talking about it. That and how much John and Betty Mae seemed to get along during this, their first meeting after their divorce. They got along so well that Patsy Kay swore up and down they would get back together. Patsy Kay also reported at the reunion that their now-grown son, a restaurant owner, had just learned that his wife was having an affair with his brother-in-law. This caused John and Betty Mae's son and daughter to get divorces and the son married the owner of another restaurant down the street. Patsy Kay's tidbits continued over the decades to fascinate.

Another person who did not attend the class reunion was Cassandra Scruggs, who was then the guest of the State while serving in its corrections facility for women. Cassandra had started clerking at the five-and-dime upon her miraculous graduation from high school and married the manager as soon as possible. When they separated she had enough money secretly squirreled away by hook and/or crook from her clerking and marriage to open a railroad salvage store out on the highway. She thought she would really make a lot of money selling all that furniture and stuff that "I can buy so cheap and then sell not so cheap, but cheap"—but just in case she needed to hit Five and Dime Manager up for some money, she was careful to delay any divorce proceedings. She seemed to prosper somewhat and bought a nice little house off the square and received appropriate sympathy when her home burned to the ground. She made a valiant recovery with the insurance money and all and bought a nice little house in Rolling Hills, hanging Boston ferns from the roof all along the side of the residence.

But things did not turn out the way she had planned and when she saw the business was going to be a total failure, she went out to the bus station and paid some transient to burn down the building (she figured for the second fire she had better be seen somewhere else while it took place) so she could get *that* insurance money. Cassandra never was too bright, and although her experience in clandestine activity had gone all the way back to Patsy Kay's aborted nuptials, she had gone out to the bus station the day after increasing the value of the policy on the building. Also, the transient reappeared a week after the fire to blackmail her for some more money. She refused to pay, so he sent a note to Sheriff Brimley. He got caught, too, what with his fingerprints all over the note, on the gasoline can, and in the FBI's fingerprint collection. Cassandra, anticipating the writing on the wall, fled to New Orleans where she hired a young lawyer from a prominent Garden District family to fight her extradition. She admitted herself to a psychiatric institution and refused contact with out-of-state detectives. After months of legal wrangling that failed to get her before a grand jury, the case became inactive and Cassandra checked herself out of the institution and left for California. There she met a wealthy retiree in his 90's whom she got to adopt her. Although handled by a sleazy ambulance-chasing lawyer in California, the New Orleans lawyer advised her through the procedure and after the old man's death the next year, Cassandra received several pieces of property and a tidy sum of money. During her stay in California she married a marine. During a visit to New Orleans while the marine was on maneuvers, she also maneuvered Young Uptown Lawyer to marry her, much to his family's horror, as Cassandra had not made her local debut. It had not occurred to his Uptown mother that he would ever marry outside the Junior League—she thought he understood that this came with that Tulane law degree she had insisted upon. Cassandra, not too keen on being around Uptown Mama by herself, went to California while Uptown Lawyer was in trial and went on vacation with the marine to Aspen, Colorado. He really enjoyed the trip and wanted to buy a bed and breakfast and retire there. While renovating the bed-and-breakfast building he purchased, Cassandra flew back to New Orleans allegedly to get some antiques on Royal Street, but in reality she was trying to spend time with Husband III to keep up the marriage front. After a couple of weeks Other Husband Uptown Lawyer had to take some depositions out of town, so she flew back to Aspen, met the hardware store manager and had him try to run her marine husband down while he was out jogging. Somehow the marine soon discovered she had never divorced Five and Dime Manager and got an annulment—somehow he did *not* discover Uptown Lawyer. Cassandra sued the marine for the deed of trust valued at $100,000 that he held on the bed and breakfast. Between Cassandra's trips to New Orleans the case file grew over a foot thick with accusations and counter accusations, and since the aforementioned marine was finding retirement was not the peaceful existence he had envisioned, he signed over the deed of trust just to be done with all things Cassandra. Although Cassandra married the hardware store manager, she flew back to New Orleans and moved in with a telephone company employee when Young Uptown Lawyer, whose specialty was maritime, flew to Greece. One day while posing in the French Quarter as a fortuneteller, Cassandra tried to get a woman she was counseling to fly to Colorado and do in the marine. The woman refused and reported the incident to the police. Cassandra came up on the computer and landed back in Addison before Young Uptown Lawyer could get back from Athens. Cassandra and the transient (mad as a hornet that Cassandra had been gallivanting all over kingdom come while he had been cooling his heels with Sheriff Brimley) were sentenced to serve maximum terms. Since Cassandra had piled up such a bunch of husbands without benefit of one divorce in this convoluted mess, everyone wondered which ones would visit her in the clink. As it turned out, none. But Patsy Kay, unable to assemble facts in any other manner, traipsed over to the jail to extend enough sympathy to Cassandra that she got the lowdown. You would have thought after catching hell from Sonny Humphrey way back in the tenth grade, Cassandra would have learned then and there that crime does not pay.

Claudia

I DON'T KNOW how Claudia met Phillip Breckenridge. I do know I had a blind date with his roommate the night he and Claudia had their first date, which was nothing spectacular. Claudia and Phillip did not go to the same college, but when she graduated they got married and James Balfour Seaton gave his second daughter a big wedding at the Methodist Church, a reception at the country club, and a honeymoon in the Smokey Mountains. He had already given her a car for college graduation since she had "not only kept her promise not to smoke until she was twenty-one, but tobacco has yet to touch her lips."

After Claudia and Phillip returned from their wedding trip, Claudia taught third grade to support them while Phillip began his second year of law school. When he graduated, they moved to Kansas for a while, but when John David Farrell, the local member of the state legislature, beckoned, they moved back to Addison and Phillip joined the firm of John David Farrell, Attorney at Law, now housed in the Farrell Building.

No one had ever doubted that John David had his eye on the governor's mansion, and when he decided to make the run, move in he did. His clients were comforted to know that the son-in-law of James Balfour Seaton would be handling their legal matters while John David was running the state.

The campaign of John David Farrell consisted of a lot of handshaking, back slapping, baby kissing, and one day a week the governor-to-be would go to work (after a fashion) at a "working man's job"—until the media had thoroughly documented the effort. He would spend the rest of the week making speeches on how he now knew the working man's problems from having had this experience. A favorite campaign picture was of John David wearing a hard hat and denim overalls and carrying a metal lunchbox. Everyone in Addison knew this was the first time The Common Man's Candidate had ever worn a hard hat and that he had not worn overalls or carried a lunchbox since that summer he measured cotton before his senior year in law school. John David took this working man's image very seriously and a major campaign decision for each week was what the next working man's job should be. John David had to work his way through college and law school and preferred to harken back to jobs he knew from the days of yore. The first week of his campaign John David scheduled a day of plowing. But John David lived a charmed life, and mercifully the rains came and the future Governor went over to Junior Sullivan's and bagged groceries until appropriate documentation was completed. The next week his luck held out again and his day of bulldozing was also "called on accounta rain." But evidently this short episode gave him enough experience to know and understand the needs of enough common men to get John David elected.

Of local interest was the fact that Billy Mike Mallory was John David's campaign manager. He lived on the family place which fronted the highway on the outskirts of the city limits. At the very edge of the property there was an easement for a road which ran the entire depth of the Mallory property until it reached the large expanse of property behind, which was the family place of the Sowell family, now headed by Joe Don Sowell. Shortly after Billy Mike acquired his campaign responsibilities, wouldn't you know that Joe Don became treasurer for John David's chief rival, who lived sixty miles away. Joe Don and Billy Mike had never gotten along—probably some feud which started in a previous generation regarding the easement, and it seemed every time Joe Don had to rush somewhere from home to get to one of the opponent's rallies or whatnot, Billy Mike always had some obstruction such as a bulldozer or tractor in the drive. There was always some excuse—mowing the huge lawn, construction of a patio—no one could ever remember Billy Mike's *ever* taking such an interest in improving his house or land. Joe Don would wheel around and go back to his house for his shotgun while somebody in Billy Mike's house called Sheriff Brimley. This routine went on throughout the campaign, and by the time the election finally arrived, Billy Mike Mallory had a house renovated from stem to stern, a manicured lawn worthy of Disneyland, and the first home swimming pool in Addison.

John David had been married to Zella forever. Few people ever saw her, and it was said she was crazy and stayed in the basement apartment of Possum Trot, their estate which was several miles out from town off the Dam Road. Since they had eight children, it was assumed they had driven her nuts. Whether they had or not, that was as good a reason as she needed to stay holed up in the basement and away from the wild bunch upstairs.

"I wish *I* had a basement where *I* could hole up from *my* four young'uns," declared Martha Louise Potter any time she was engaged in the gossip the Farrells inspired. Zella's condition was looked upon as the reason for which John David's roving eye was excused by all but the most hard-shelled members of the Enlightened Morning Star Baptist Church.

His most frequent companion was young enough to be one of his many daughters. He had taken up with Maureen during his last campaign and had seemed to have genuine affection for her. Her father was Frank Heflin, the most successful used car dealer in the county, who had said nothing when Maureen was seen driving around town in a brand-new red Cadillac convertible. None of the townsfolk doubted where it had come from—and they were right. Heflin had never thought his daughter capable of catching anyone like John David, and he would never protest her being involved with a married man when the married man was John David Farrell. After all, he might need John David's influence or political favors at any given time, being involved as he was in the illegal gambling operation hidden out in the open at the reservoir.

John David and Maureen discreetly kept company in a small modern house he rented for her out on Birddog Road, which forked off from the main drag to the reservoir. One night after the election as they were discussing the way in which he would fill the various positions at his disposal, the matter of his social obligations came up. Since he and Maureen were not married and Zella was not about to come out of the basement, some sort of arrangement for entertaining had to be decided which would be acceptable to the Enlightened Ladies and the rest of the ultra-conservative voters in the state. Maureen, a very bright, pretty young lady with a long thick mane of auburn hair, immediately thought of my mother to be his hostess. John David thought that was a brilliant idea.

My mother, then retired, after selling her shop had taught English and music to the last two generations of Addison and had them, even the football players—who were indeed the conference champions, sing in the living Christmas tree in the center of the town square every December. She was loved by everyone—to include the football players, and had a reputation as an interesting conversationalist and could put anyone, no matter how nervous, at ease. Maureen, one of her former students, had felt particularly close my mother, and when the whispers regarding her relationship with John David would distress her, she would come to our house for coffee. Mother was the soul of discretion and a completely non-condemning audience. Maureen had found refuge in Mother's home.

Mother had lived alone for a number of years and since her beloved sister resided so close to the state capital, she could live with her and commute to the governor's mansion. No one could possibly attach any scandal to the choice. John David, always very thoughtful of my mother, made it clear if she tried it and didn't want to do it, she could quit. Just like that. Quit and go home to Addison where she now lived in the old family house on Maple Street.

I remember how Mother went into a quandary when Maureen came over for coffee and brought up the offer. Mother, being a staunch Republican, had not voted for John David since a real, live Republican had actually run for Governor. She thought it would be dishonest if she accepted. When she called me in New Orleans and told me about this unbelievable turn of events, I was delighted for her, encouraged the move, and thought it was a hoot that she ever worried about not voting for John David and receiving his guests. "After all, Mother, it's a secret ballot." Her conscience got the best of her and when she told Maureen she did not vote for John David, Maureen exploded with laughter, as did John David when it was passed on to him. The offer still stood.

The inauguration of John David Farrell took place on the coldest January day anyone could remember. Snow, so rare in the state capital that no equipment had ever been purchased for its removal, began to swirl around the majorettes, wearing little more than their goose bumps at the front of the Addison High School Band leading the parade down Capital Avenue. Everyone in the town of Addison thought it was a fine gesture on John David's part to have the Addison High School Band lead his way to the Capitol, especially since he personally paid the band's expenses for the trip. Martha Louise commended the Governor—"Not one cakewalk had to be held, not one car had to be washed, not one booth had to be manned in the square. Good ol' John David!"

That night at the glittering Governor's Ball, John David welcomed the best-dressed voters in the state—none of whom wore hard hats—and reassured them once again, as he had during his speech earlier in the day, that he was all the state would need to solve its problems and climb to heights of prosperity never known. Phillip had even bought Claudia a mink jacket for the occasion.

Maureen, radiantly beautiful in the green strapless evening gown she had gone to Memphis to find, discreetly stayed out of the spotlight, her pride and love for the Governor evident only in her eyes as she gazed at him from across the room. She had gathered her wild curls and smoothed them into a sophisticated but soft chignon with only wisps of auburn framing her face—along with the stunning emerald and diamond earrings that she had found on her pillow after John David departed the first morning they had breakfast in the condo. True to his word, he had brought her with him to the state capital. Upon arrival he purchased the penthouse condo in Palace Place and presented her with the deed, which was in her name. He had had to stay in his hotel suite all this week—the press and his aides had barely left him time to sleep alone, much less nurture their relationship. Everyone wanted to know whom he wanted to appoint to what; those few who did not just wanted to be appointed. She had seen him in her official capacities left over from the campaign, and though their affair was the worst-kept secret in the administration, no one could question her professionalism or her role as a definite asset to the Governor-elect. They had not had a moment alone together, and John David appreciated but was not surprised that she had asked nothing of him. She never did. Yes, he loved her. He needed her by his side. One day he would marry her, but that would have to wait for now. His quest for the governor's chair had taken precedence over everything else. And after four years maybe there would be a run for the U. S. Senate.

That Zella stayed holed up in the basement was good and it was bad. It was good that she was out of sight, along with the booze and the screaming fits she threw every time John David tried to coax her out. Even though she was a captive of her own wild reasoning, she knew he wanted out of the marriage. She would not come out and do anything that would give him an excuse to dump her. Look at what she had accomplished from the basement—why, she was the First Lady of the state! She had not helped her husband campaign. Not a smidgen. She had not been on display at his side—not for a single picture. She had not even emerged to vote for her husband on Election Day. And the kids! One of the perks she would enjoy as First Lady was having them out of the house, miles away in the state capital! No more having to let them in to see her. She would stay in the house outside of Addison, with Ellie May Brown serving her meals and doing her laundry and cleaning up after her. Ellie May's husband Ronald would keep the grounds pretty and the house fixed up. Now she would even have the Governor's security people keeping the neighbors away. She could drink and watch her soaps in peace.

While Zella was holed up in the basement of the house outside Addison, the First Children were there with their daddy for his inauguration, ordering the staff of the mansion around as fast as they could think up the next wish to be granted. John David's proud mama had seen to it that the girls were all turned out in ruffles and bows, the boys all wearing long pants. Yes, it was quite a night!

Years later Claudia, who had kept me posted in all things, said, "Never in my wildest dreams did I ever think my whole future would be tied to John David Farrell's star!" Since his ascent to the governor's chair had prompted John David to anoint Phillip to act in his stead in the law firm, Phillip began to receive attention he had never thought would be his. Suddenly he was catapulted into the big-league practice of law. A force to be reckoned with statewide—after all, he had the Governor's ear. Or so it was perceived.

Just as suddenly Claudia was catapulted into the role of the wife of a high-profile lawyer. Although her father had been a well-to-do, generous parent and always there for her, she now was spending a lot of money that had not come from him. The allowance from her trust fund became reinvested rather than spent to supplement her husband's income. She also found herself in the unexpected role of Hostess for a Powerhouse Attorney. She had to entertain. She had to plan dinner parties. She was already a whiz at bridge.

She was determined to do whatever was necessary to keep her husband in the forefront of his profession. Although shy all her life, she plunged into the social swim and excelled at executing the most imaginative of evening buffets, afternoon teas, and various other hen parties. All this while carrying within her body one child or another. Phillip didn't keep her barefoot, but he did keep her pregnant. Born in succession were Jamie Balfour, Rebecca Lynn, Olivia Roselie, and Little Phillip.

Claudia was a devoted mother and despite her heavy social calendar, her children always came first, and she conscientiously chaired PTA committees, worked the concession stand for the benefit of the high school band at football games, carpooled, took various children to the orthodontist in Memphis, had everyone all scrubbed and beribboned for Sunday School, had every child to the appropriate music lesson at Miss Effie's on time, all homework checked for the next day, and stayed up all night with the sick child du jour.

Phillip, having benefited from John David's prudently naming James Balfour Seaton's son-in-law as his voice in absentia, basked in the limelight. He wallowed in it. It never occurred to him to wonder why John David would call him from out of the blue, pluck him from obscurity in Kansas, and right there over the phone offer him, sight unseen, the chance of a lifetime.

Eventually Claudia and Phillip decided to buy a lot in Crown Estates. After planning their house, they had to buy the lots on both sides, so large was their house to be. Claudia never knew how much Phillip was making, she just knew that no matter how much she spent, he paid the bills. She had never seen an insurance policy and when their annual tax return was placed before her for signature, she just signed her name without reading any of it. Phillip did not veto a single thing she planned for the house. Each of the children was to have his/her own room with bath. Phillip would have an exercise room. Claudia was to have a study with big-screen television for her soap-opera watching. Phillip never asked how much any of these plans would cost. He just wrote the checks.

Claudia spent hours on the road to Memphis, where she canvassed the city finding just the right fabrics, just the right wallpaper, just the right fixtures. When it was time to have their first open house, the whole town—except for Zella Farrell—flocked to visit "Mr. and Mrs. Phillip Breckenridge, At Home, 4:00 p.m.-6:00 p.m., Sunday, May 6."

Much to Phillip's relief, Governor John David Farrell flew up from the state capital. Of course John David knew a lot of people would show up in order to see him, and John David did not disappoint. It was the very first time a helicopter had ever landed in Addison, so that was an exciting event in itself—almost as exciting as the landing of Robert E. Hall of Memphis a generation before. By the time John David was ready to go back to the capital, word had gotten around and the whole town was out in Sam Broom's cow pasture to see that chopper rise.

Claudia had the event catered by Memphis' own Delbert Worthington. Even the doctor's wife had never done that. The bridge ladies searched desperately for anything to criticize but came away with their silent mouths hanging open. The shy little girl whom the senior citizens remembered had grown up to be the wife of a very successful lawyer; she was a social and civic leader in the community, a prominent member of the Methodist Church, and now she was mistress of the most beautiful home any of them had ever imagined. She seemed to revel in it. No doubt about it, the second daughter of James Balfour Seaton was the Grande Dame of Addison.

Although John David accomplished a great deal on behalf of the citizens of the state, hardly anyone ever knew one of the greatest accomplishments of the Farrell Administration—keeping The Secret. Claudia was one of the handful of people who ever knew it, so I was soon one of the chosen few. John David's achievement actually took place while the Governor was in the hospital flat on his back with appendicitis. Or so it was thought.

Only his closest aides—and my mother—were aware that while John David and Maureen were having an entirely innocent dinner one night in the mansion, in staggered an entirely drunk Zella. She had barely gotten by security, so disheveled was she that only Talbert Dinkins from Addison, to whom John David owed a favor and was thus hired as a security officer at the gate, recognized her and had her admitted. She had climbed the grand staircase no doubt with great difficulty, and having finally succeeded, she just started opening doors at random. One of the doors was that of the private study where John David and Maureen were dining from tv trays during a break while working on some legislation.

They were watching the news and although they were startled by Zella's entrance, John David rose to welcome Zella and invited her to join their dinner. It was never known if Zella knew of John David's liaison with Maureen—Zella's reign over her kingdom in the basement did not allow for many local bulletins—but the sight of her husband with the young beauty immediately enraged the unstable Zella, and before anyone could move, Zella had gone to the serving table and grabbed a convenient, very sharp knife before raising the blade and heading straight for Maureen's flaming tresses. John David leaped at once to stop Zella as her arm came down wielding the blade. It went straight into the Governor's body right below his belt buckle.

Maureen's scream pierced the stately silence of the mansion, but before his guards could reach him, John David had taken another stab in the abdomen. They found him in a pool of blood, with Maureen struggling with his crazed wife. Zella was restrained and locked in a nearby bedroom. John David was rushed to the nearest hospital with Maureen at his side, holding his hand and whispering reassurances to him which he could not hear. The hospital was alerted that secrecy was to be maintained and when the flashing lights caught the attention of the press, their inquiries went unanswered. The oxygen mask over John David's face prevented his identification upon arrival in the emergency room, and he was quickly sequestered privately. A team of surgeons marched into the operating theatre to save the life of the Governor of the state. It was quickly decided that the Governor's appendix should be removed in addition to the repair necessitated by Zella's intrusion, and when the press blackout was lifted, that was all that was announced. The Governor had merely been admitted for an emergency appendectomy. An unquiet Zella was quietly placed in a very private mental institution a few miles away. Maureen never left her vigil, first outside the operating room, then in and out of intensive care, later at the Governor's side in his private suite. When John David regained consciousness he looked up into her anxious face, and with her dark, unkempt auburn hair making an aura around her face from the light behind her, he was certain he had died.

"Are you and angel? Am I in heaven?" he inquired.

Maureen was so startled as his question broke the intense concern she had endured over the past two days that she burst into hysterical laughter. "Not with *your* record, Guv! You'll never get past the devil!"

Although Mother never took the job at the Mansion, she remained the confidant of the person closest to the Governor. Between Maureen's chats with my mother and Claudia's reports which she never knew supplemented other reports to me, I wondered if I didn't know more about the running of the state than anyone but John David and Maureen.

When John David Farrell had served his term as Governor he was unable to succeed himself and came back to Addison to be an elder statesman while he decided if he wanted to run for the United States Senate.

Settling down in Addison, John David moved into the plush office which had been kept reserved only for him during his tenure in the state capital (although Phillip had enjoyed sitting in John David's chair late at night when he was at the firm alone—except for Jessie Maynard, his immensely loyal receptionist, who always volunteered to stay late when an attorney did "so you won't be bothered by the phone." She was such a helpful little thing.

Upon John David's return, Phillip found himself all but ignored by those who had courted him so conscientiously for four years, and he silently seethed in his much smaller office. Now he had to actually direct his attention to clients who had accidents as he pursued the practice of law. Jessie provided a willing ear, and Phillip more than appreciated her understanding.

It did not take long for the tension to erupt, and Phillip blew up one day at John David and, seizing his briefcase, stormed out the door. Claudia dutifully stood by him during the ruckus which followed and rented the vacant building right off the square so Phillip could set up his own practice. Claudia dipped into the trust fund Mr. Seaton had established for her and spent thousands of dollars on computers, a copy machine, and other office essentials while she set up the office herself. She bought a telephone system and brought in her mother to set up the accounting procedures. Mrs. Seaton enjoyed showing this expertise and receiving compliments about how her daughter put the firm together—the whole town was talking about it. The entire family pitched in and Phillip found himself practicing law by the end of the month.

Claudia hired a secretary for Phillip and was there at the firm every day bright and early in her capacity as business and office manager. She found it a welcome relief from the bridge table, a pastime she felt she need not pursue now that John David had arrived home to roost and Phillip had cut the cord. She had not worked since before her first child and loved the feeling of accomplishment she had at the end of each day. In establishing the office, she could look around and actually see the fruits of her labor, and since her daddy had been making some phone calls, the clients were beginning to trickle in.

Phillip also seemed to look at Mrs. Seaton's daughter in a new light. He was very proud of what she had done and was generous in his praise of her when speaking to others. He did not hide his astonishment in the discovery of her business talent and acumen, and this was the subject of much good-natured kidding.

One day I called Claudia from New Orleans to find that she was "at home today." I called her there, and asked how the Captain of Industry was doing.

"Not so well," she replied quietly.

"Oh? What's the matter?" I thought she might be sick.

There was a silence. Then, "Phillip and I are getting a divorce."

I was shocked beyond words. "Phillip tried to throw me out of the house, but I thought, 'Why should *I* be the one to leave'—I told him if he didn't want us to be married, he could be single elsewhere. *I* was staying. He started having a fling with the secretary I hired for him. He can have *her* and I'll have the house.

"I should have known—I hired Jessie Maynard."

"What??" I was in disbelief.

"Well," responded Claudia, "I had a very narrow choice. It was either her or Lucy Clanton."

Claudia was getting the older girls ready for college, and they liked putting on their applications that a whole law firm bore the name of their daddy alone. That would no doubt look good on their applications for rush, too—sororities liked to pledge girls whose parents could pay. There was no need to say daddy was the only attorney in the firm.

If one of the girls went to the University, it was very important that she pledge either Tri Delt, Chi O, or KD. Phillip had gone to law school there and he knew.

I well remember when Sallybeth went over there, as Hally said thoughtfully, "Her mama's gonna kill her dead on the floor if she pledges anything else!"

So we other nine fervently hoped one of the three would offer Sallybeth a bid while her mama called every Tri Delt, Chi O, or KD alum she had ever heard of in order to get proper recommendations to membership chairmen by rush. Mrs. Waltrip had it all planned—Sallybeth would pledge (preferably) Chi O so she could be elected cheerleader her freshman year; her sophomore year Sallybeth would be in the Parade of Beauties; as a junior she had to be elected a favorite, so her senior year she could be Miss University. During this time prime stock from the most prestigious families in the state would parade to the family home in Addison to be inspected. Mrs. Waltrip, completely ignoring the fact Sallybeth wanted to be feature twirler, then drum major of the University band—not a cheerleader—and was going steady with Jimmie Gayle Trambeau, was adamant that Sallybeth would marry into one of the prominent clans sponsoring their sons at the University in some lucrative endeavor like the study of law or medicine.

This was not necessary in the case of Lucinda Marshall, since she and Trey Justice had gone steady since Lucinda had moved to Addison in the sixth grade.

Trey had made a significant contribution to the social life in Addison, because when he played at Addison High, the football team gave us another nucleus for activity besides the church. Having the cheerleaders yell and scream as the team burst onto the field got to be compulsory, even for the out-of-town games, and the band had to blare away with us majorettes strutting and posing until the whole thing erupted with Trey's grand entrance. We started having majorette-cheerleader suppers right before the home games, and since no one could attend who was not in one group or the other, we envisioned that we had a sort of an elite status, even among The Twelve. Our mothers saw to it that we dined on sumptuous, pretty food and our tables were decorated with school colors and flowers. We band members were especially smug—after all, while all the cheerleaders could do was jump around and holler, we majorettes in the fine Southern tradition could *twirl*.

Meanwhile, the football team was taking the pre-game ritual more seriously. They marched solemnly into the school cafeteria with its spartan, severe environment of stainless steel and concrete and began the serious business of devouring dry roast beef and boiled potatoes with nothing on them ("The coach don't want us eatin' grease before the game.") along with scorched toast, without even marmalade to inspire interest. They would sit and shovel in the parched food with very few words spoken and rise to go to the gym, knowing this was a sacrifice they had endured in order to be the state champions. They did not want to lose a game because somebody sneaked in marmalade. There would be plenty of time for marmalade during the off season after the State Championship Football trophy had been securely placed in all its glory in the trophy case outside Miss Greenway's classroom.

As the team kept winning and Trey got famous statewide, the momentum grew as the season went on and just having a game at home was reason enough to have the band parade through the town square on Friday afternoons heralding the event. Trey's star power was indirectly contagious, as the majorettes and cheerleaders appeared so much that we started getting photographed ourselves for the school paper and *The Addisonian*. But by that time Trey's picture was making regular appearances in the Memphis *Commercial Appeal* and the paper in the state capital.

Homecoming with our expectant-looking queen was bigger that year than ever before, since by then we knew Trey would probably get us the state title. The floats depleted the entire town's stock of crepe paper before they were finished—but Martha Louise Potter volunteered to make an emergency run to Memphis in her station wagon on Wednesday and saved the day. What with all the college coaches coming around, Brown's Cafe was a lively place on Fridays before the game and then on Saturday when the men in town would gather to rehash the game. On Monday the entire weekend was reviewed from the farmers' early-morning coffee to the lunch special—the game, the coaches, and did Trey's mama see Coach So-and-So from Thus-and-Such College at morning services at the Enlightened Morning Star Baptist Church.

It did not take Trey long to carry the University team to a national ranking. Lucinda wasn't particularly interested in pursuing a collegiate career, but she did want to keep tabs on Trey, so she dabbled in Chi O to which she easily got a bid when her connection to Trey Justice was publicized the first day of rush—she was careful to wear his enormous high school class ring riding high on her breast, dangling as it was from a bright red ribbon around her neck. It really stood out on that virginal white frock. Lucinda played bridge in the grill and majored in a different subject every semester. This well-rounded education soon became tiresome, but she hung in there until Trey's senior year. Lucinda and Trey would be rich, which hardly seemed fair since their rise to the brass (or in Lucinda's case, diamond) ring all just came so *effortlessly*. He would even be famous without Lucinda's lifting a finger. Her mama had just let Lucinda bide her time and waited to be told when to plan the wedding, which would be no later than the NFL draft his senior year. As soon as University beat State, Trey ambled in to Roberson's Jewelers and walked out with a huge diamond engagement ring for one of the fingers Lucinda would never have to lift. Tad Roberson knew Trey was going to be worth millions—he could wait for the ring to be paid off in view of all the other jewelry he knew Lucinda would expect. Trey was voted MVP in the bowl game his senior year, and professional scouts were salivating. The draft came and went and Trey was selected in the first round. Right on cue Marsha Marshall got out her pad and pen and called her cousin Sachet Biggs at Flowers by Squench. The remaining members of The Twelve met to plan The Shower.

Although Trey's home team would be out of state, Marsha and Leslie assured that Trey knew to bring their daughter home in the off season—and to retire to Addison—when they gave the children a big lot in Rolling Hills for a wedding present. As soon as the couple got back from their honeymoon in Gatlinburg and rented an apartment near the team's practice field, Lucinda had to hurry back to Addison so she and Marsha could go see Tommy Roberson about the house plans. Trey made the starting lineup and everything was B-movie perfect until he got tackled by Bronco Tuminella and was carried off the field, never to return. When he and Lucinda moved back to town, the house in Rolling Hills was finished and Rodney Tidwell was already putting down mulch. Trey did not care about the mulch but he did care about pursuing business interests in Memphis and kept his good leg on the accelerator while his Cadillac flew past Graceland about three times a week. He kept his interests private until Wilma Sykes saw him in the fur department at Goldsmith's and told Lucinda to expect that mink coat. When Lucinda's great expectation came to naught, Leslie hired a private detective from Memphis, who did not have far to go since the first time he tailed Trey they wound up at Cleopatra's Barge, a cheap night club right off Beale Street. There Vincent Palermo, P.I., saw Francine La Tour ("Just let your eyes tour her body") doing the most exotic belly dance he had ever imagined while Trey sat in one of the elevated back booths with his glass of Rebel Yell.

Teebo called me long distance from Maryland after receiving the news from his source. He swore up and down The Source had personally spoken to Palermo as well as read the actual report Palermo turned in to Leslie.

According to Teebo, Francine could put Salome to shame, and when her undulating was over, she made a bee-line for Trey, who rose to embrace her and what few veils covered her richly-endowed torso. The passionate kiss she returned was accompanied by gyrations against his body while his hands explored her sculptured curves. Palermo, along with everyone else in the dimly-lit joint, thought Trey would finish stripping her right there, but she pulled teasingly away and led him by the hand through the beaded curtains.

"He must have done a lot of research to find this one," breathed Palermo to himself, "She's a real pistol!" He wondered how he had missed this spectacular specimen of womankind during all his prowls in Memphis' sleazy bars—this was the kind of thing he was on the lookout for all the time—something to put between his sheets when he packed it in right before dawn. He appreciated a fully-developed female more than anyone he knew, and this one had been only a few blocks from his office. He had better pay more attention—he had been neglecting his home turf. Surely there was other treasure to be had. Really had. Or maybe he would just wait until Trey was through with Francine.

Palermo strolled out to his car and opened the crowded trunk to get the camera with the telescopic lens. He had checked the marquee and Francine had another show in two hours. She and Trey were probably screwing somewhere in the back and he would maybe stay for the next show; Palermo would be there to record everything. He crossed the street and slipped up the alley by the bar. At the end of the building there was a solid-core door which Palermo was surprised to find ajar. It screamed as he pried it further open and squeezed into the darkness. Just as he got inside, he stumbled on some beer bottles and fell against a stack of boxes which crashed to the sticky floor.

Palermo cursed under his breath as he jumped into a shadow to conceal his entrance. The deafening rhythm of the tinny music in the bar covered the sound of the cascading boxes, and after waiting two or three minutes, Palermo was satisfied he had not been discovered and proceeded to inch his way down the hall. No one appeared as he slipped along the dirty brick wall. Around the corner he saw a faded star on a badly-scarred door.

"Must be Cleo's lair," he thought to himself, "and paydirt!" He crept toward the breathless moans from within and, satisfied that he heard Trey enjoying Cleo, Palermo quietly made his way back into the alley. He went back out into the street and circling the block, on the other side of the building he found a fence which he had no trouble vaulting. There was the window to Francine's dressing room and a big fat finder's fee! Thus began the surveillance of Trey and the Queen of the Nile.

By the time Leslie got through with Mr. All America, Trey had coughed up the house, $800,000, and a new car per year for the next ten years. He did not know what hit him. The ladies of the Enlightened Morning Star Baptist Church just could not say how horrified they were that a man they had known since the day he was born would go and carry on with that belly dancer from Memphis. They could not, but they tried—tried at ladies circle, tried at prayer meeting, and tried at Bible study twice a week. Martha Louise Potter had so many bridge parties that Junior Sullivan over at the grocery store ran out of potato chips twice. No one knew when there would be another scandal to match this one, so it was milked for all it was worth.

But Trey came through for them one more time—he actually *married* the belly dancer. No one could believe it, especially his Enlightened mama, who would not allow the family name to be disgraced by having it along with that of Francine La Tour (née Thelma Delma Beard) on the same engraved wedding invitation. So Trey and Francine were married without fanfare at the city hall in Memphis. They built a big house out in the country and Trey supervised a fertile farm when he was not traveling around recruiting for the University football team and occasionally scouting for the NFL team that drafted him.

Everyone in town said if he had not been hurt he would have led his team to the Super Bowl. We all knew this was true—after all, Addison's high school football team had not even been conference champions since Trey graduated.

The Enlightened Ladies decided they needed something to do besides play bridge, and since there was never enough church-going accomplished, they decided to add extra Bible Study to the ferris wheel of religious activities. What really got me was that Bible Study was every day. Then they got to thinking about the ladies who worked during business hours, so another Bible Study was added at night. No one outside the membership was ever told what went on there (which made me wonder how potential members knew whether or not to join). Outsiders just assumed the ladies did indeed study the Bible. But if that were so, what were they hiding? Why was it a secret—"Go ye therefore" and all. The ladies who worked at the hosiery mill and did not belong day or night called it The Cult.

Then there was the Garden Club. There were yards in Addison that would have put landscapes in *Better Homes and Gardens* to shame. Mrs. Trotter, however, usually got the "Yard of the Month" and the honor of displaying the sign. She always had a neat, pretty yard, which featured a little round minnow pond about four feet in diameter, which was ringed with white brick and had a tiny white bridge from one side to the other. The "Yard of the Month" sign was always posted to the right of it. It looked like tree bark with lime green lettering heralding "Yard of the Month"—that is, until she scandalized the Garden Ladies (most of whom were also Enlightened) by actually *painting* their lovely sign black and white!

A special emergency meeting of the Garden Club was held when Mildred Simms first saw "the monstrosity" right there by Mrs. Trotter's famous minnow pond. The honor that month was rescinded and a special vote was taken that Mrs. Trotter could never again have "Yard of the Month" no matter how many weeds she pulled, leaves she raked, or mulch she put down. Observed Martha Louise Potter, "It should have gone to the Draper sisters anyway. Everybody knows it was just mean-spirited politics that gave Miz Trotter the honor that month."

Jasmine Draper had stolen Sis Tutwiler's boyfriend from her when they were in the third grade; it mattered not that Mrs. Tutwiler had just celebrated her fiftieth wedding anniversary with her next suitor. Mrs. Tutwiler had marshaled support from the Enlightened Ladies and defeated Jasmine's forces which were the few Presbyterians and members of the Methodist Church. The two ladies from the Church of Christ had abstained.

Letitia

LETITIA BECAME HEAD cheerleader our junior year. With that exception, Letitia was a behind-the-scenes kind of person and Bonnie was always up front—she was usually president of her class. Bonnie usually got whatever job or honor Letitia had left behind when she went to the next grade or graduated—they were both, in turn, editor of the school paper. As children, their home was a gathering place for neighborhood kids, and since they lived next door to their grandparents, we had double the yard space in which to play.

When she went to college, Letitia came home from the University every weekend, and one Friday afternoon, Perry Whitestone, who had always been a good friend of hers, came by to say good-bye, as he had just joined the service and was going to the orient. He was our age, and they sat in the swing on the front porch and talked about his going overseas. One thing led to another I guess, and on the spur of the moment, Perry asked Letitia to marry him and meet him in the Philippines. She said okay but was hesitant to go tell her mother, so she told Bonnie instead. Bonnie said she would go with her to break the news, since there was safety in numbers and she had just found out she was pregnant. She had neglected to ever divulge to the family that she and Satchel Hawkins from Mount Olive had gotten married seven months before, but this unexpected turn of events necessitated her 'fessing up. Bessie and Junior Sullivan were really knocked for a loop, but what with getting a wedding together for Letitia by the next afternoon, they did not have much time to raise any hell. The town heard about this newsworthy event at church on Sunday when Letitia did not show up to play the organ and Quimby Sylvester had to substitute and sightread everything from "Holy, Holy, Holy" to "The Doxology." The Sullivans were Methodists, and since Patsy Kay was over at the Enlightened Morning Star Baptist Church where Brother Fox always held forth until at least one o'clock, she did not hear about it for almost two hours. But she went into her emergency overdrive and was out at Shug's by three with all pertinent information. You had to give Patsy Kay credit—her reconnaissance was amazing.

Bessie and Junior called Spike Trammel to clear any legal hurdles about waiting periods and what-not, and Elmo Tidmore—ever prepared now since John August had given the word "impromptu" unprecedented urgency—went right over to the house to perform the ceremony. He arrived just after Sachet Biggs came in with the flowers she had put together to go on Miz Lula Thompson's grave. Fortunately, Mrs. Thompson's son Herman had just told Sachet to put flowers on her tombstone every year on her birthday, and it was wonderful luck that ol' Miz Thompson had died just two weeks ago, in time for this birthday. With Bonnie as her matron of honor, Letitia became Mrs. Whitestone at four o'clock that Saturday afternoon, "at the home of the bride, before immediate family." Cake was served on the big round dining room table along with lime sherbet floating in ginger ale, with the dead Miz Thompson's birthday flowers having been moved in from the living-room nuptials to provide an appropriate centerpiece. Following the ceremony, the couple rode up to Memphis for a wedding night at the Peabody and Sachet Biggs took the wedding/reception/birthday flowers—which had certainly given their money's worth—to the cemetery in time for the deceased Mrs. Thompson's birthday. Perry left from the Millington naval station to defend our country in Manila, and the plan was for Letitia to finish out the semester at the University and then join him at his post.

That left Bonnie and her newly-revealed husband to move in over at her grandmother's. This was a The Shower that The Twelve did not have to give, but Marsha Marshall and Lucinda gave a fine one at Lucinda's house, since there it sat all new and barely used. The Enlightened Ladies Et Al arrived in droves all prepared to be so happy for the bride's good fortune, but after seeing the opulence which Trey had bestowed upon Lucinda, joy was harder to come by than dark green envy. But beautiful silver and crystal and china were displayed, and the young couple was prepared to dine in fine style.

Bonnie gave birth to beautiful little Deborah over the summer, enrolled at the University that fall, and commuted while her grandmother and a doting aunt took care of the baby. True to form, Bonnie made the dean's list every semester, got her master's, and eventually got a doctorate in education. Letitia and Perry traveled the globe while he was in the service, and all the civic organizations in town got their mothers to speak after each visit to see them, as so few people in the county had been abroad except the veterans in time of war. This also allowed for going-away parties, welcome-home parties, and various ladies lunches to hear the news of the children.

Junior never ran out of potato chips, not even once.

One Sunday night our junior year in high school, the cars started gathering at the telephone booth. All headlights were trained on it while the Presbyterian youth waited for their Methodist counterparts. I was in Teebo's car with Hally and Claudia. When about twelve cars were present, Jimmie Gayle scratched off and the caravan headed for the stop light. Just as we got there it turned red, and everyone jumped out of the cars as was customary on Sunday nights, ran around them, and jumped back in before the light changed. Jimmie Gayle led us in a loop by Shug's, circled three times, and not seeing much potential for interest there, he wheeled around and headed for the Dam Road.

There was a stretch of pavement that was called "The Quarter" just over the first little bridge on the Dam Road. It was marked just after the bridge and then a quarter-mile later. It was the drag strip for the guys, who would race two at a time to see whose family car could, from a dead stop, get to the highest speed by the second marker. It was always used the first Sunday night after any parents got a new car. Since the Dam Road was only two lanes wide, there was the added excitement if another car were approaching from the other direction. Since no one had been killed yet, we knew better than any parents that the cars of Addison were a lot better than they had ever dreamed. There were no new cars in our entourage, so Jimmie Gayle did not stop at The Quarter and we followed in hot pursuit, which got hotter as Jimmie Gayle pressed harder on his accelerator, and before long we were on top of the dam, lights switched off, flirting with oblivion. When all cars had successfully crossed the dam, the line switched lights on and headed back to town. We assumed.

But Jimmie Gayle was our leader and turned off on a gravel road about three miles on the way back. We followed the cloud of dust, wondering where it would take us. A few miles later Jimmie Gayle took another turn, this time on to a narrow dirt road. Even he slowed down.

"Oh, no!" Teebo muttered. "He's headed for Beau Rivage!"

"Why in the world would he go out *there*?" Hally asked. This is ridiculous! In the dead of night—"

"Don't say 'dead'," Teebo cautioned, "but we can't turn back."

We had slowed down much more than we usually did during our Sunday night follow-the-leader escapades, but before long we reached the field by Beau Rivage. We pulled up behind Jimmie Gayle's car which he had parked to the side of the road, but Teebo kept our headlights on and the motor running. Jimmie Gayle got out of his car holding a flashlight and ambled over to Teebo, who rolled down his window.

"Man, are you ka-RAzy?" Teebo asked without ceremony. "We're on the backside of nowhere!"

"Listen," Jimmie Gayle said seriously, "I was over here hunting the other day and there were some rays of light coming from the ruins. Going straight up. And I heard some moaning. I thought someone might be hurt or something so I started walking over there. Then I heard a faint sound of—what sounded like drums."

"Oh, come on, Jimmie Gayle. Nobody's gonna buy that," said Teebo.

"No, it's true. I swear. There didn't seem to be anyone here, but when I heard the drums it sounded like a lot of them, but a very faint sound—like a hundred drums, but right in the ruin."

"Jimmie Gayle, the ruin couldn't hold a hundred anything—except maybe rats!" Hally informed.

"That's another thing that was so peculiar—" Jimmie Gayle said thoughtfully, "it's just not big enough. But I called out and it stopped. Just like that. It was totally quiet. I called out again, and then I thought I'd better get the hell out of here. But now there are a lot of us."

"Oh, yeah. More to die. Get us all killed at one time. Very efficient," Teebo mumbled. He had a way of getting to the heart of matters.

The other cars began to line up behind us, with some of the kids getting out. Considering the location, some of them stayed behind. Jimmie Gayle gave a motion like John Wayne summoning the wagon train to follow and headed toward the ruin. Several of the guys had the presence of mind to bring flashlights, but most of us did not have one so we kept close together. Betty Mae complained about runs in her hose—we were all dressed for church and not for hiking in dark country fields—but we girls knew on Sunday nights any girl along was just one of the guys. No sissy comments.

"Oh, shut up Betty Mae," someone said in the darkness. "If you come, you have to be a sport."

"No I don't," she retorted.

"Then go get back in the car." That shut her up.

"She oughtta be worryin' about chigger bites. Chiggers and ticks are gonna be a much larger concern than a run in her stupid hose," muttered Teebo. "I don't reckon any of y'all girls happen to carry coal oil around in those purses, do you?"

I had not thought about chiggers. I had never been bitten by a tick, but chiggers were a different matter! After getting bitten very badly by these microscopic varmints one summer when my mother took some of us little children blueberry picking, I could certainly appreciate what Teebo was saying—I had even had to go to the doctor! I thought chigger bites were worse than chicken pox or measles.

"I think I'd rather encounter the ghost of Beau Rivage than chiggers," I said breathlessly.

"Careful, Margie," cautioned Claudia, struggling to keep up, "we don't want the ghosts to think they're *invited*!"

The moon was full and we could see the dark hulk of the ruin as we approached it. Most of the walls had crumbled, but there were three or four that had strong sections and they were still standing. The weeds and brush were prolific, but we kept on going, hoping Jimmie Gayle would turn back—but fat chance of that. Teebo was leading Hally and me, and we had been joined by Claudia and Trey Justice. I actually was not too scared with Jimmie Gayle, Dex, Teebo, and Trey along. But as we trudged in the moonlight, I would much have preferred to be back in town at Betty Mae's listening to Dan Crockett recite *Peyton Place* while Elvis sang "Only Fools Rush In" on one of Betty Mae's jillion 45's. It crossed my mind that right now Elvis was referring to *us*.

We got close to the remains of the building. Dex, right behind our pioneering Jimmie Gayle, called softly, "Y'all watch where you step, you hee-yuh?" Dex had picked up Southern idioms very quickly. "There're some rotten beams here and you might fall over 'em. And part of the floor has rotted, too. Don't fall in."

With that bit of encouragement, Teebo extended his hand from an elevated bit of stone and pulled me up even with Beau Rivage.

It was so very quiet. A soft summer breeze was blowing and moving some of the leaves in the trees, but there was no sound at all. Just the dark fragment of an old mansion bathed in moonlight. Everyone was now up on the level of the house and Jimmie Gayle and Dex went within its boundaries. We could not see much of anything, but most of us crowded close to a wall that looked sturdy. We were being careful to try not to get hurt. We knew if anything happened to anyone, we would never hear the end of it. And we *never* wanted to have to explain our Sunday nights.

There were about ten of us really close together, and when Claudia lost her footing, she fell back against the group and that pushed Trey up against a wall. To our surprise, he fell right through! He hollered as the wall collapsed, and Betty Mae, who was very good at it, screamed bloody murder. We were all astonished that the wall had given way, and we were scared there might be such things as ghosts after all.

Jimmie Gayle and Dex lunged forward to help Trey, while the flashlights trained on the hole, and I heard Jimmie Gayle say, "What in the—"

We heard Dex ask Trey if he were all right and were relieved to hear him say, "Yeah—where is this? What're those?"

"It's a secret room," Teebo announced.

"Books," replied Jimmie Gayle. "Books and books and books."

"This isn't a room," Trey said. "It's a closet."

"It couldn't be a closet," I volunteered, "back during the Civil War no one *had* closets. People were taxed by how many rooms they had and a closet was considered a room. That's why we all have old armoires from back then."

I was trying to see in. So was everybody else. For the moment we had forgotten to be afraid. Sure enough, the space continued for several feet beyond.

"Look at all these books," Jimmie Gayle said, his voice still registering amazement.

I looked inside. There were several bookcases totally laden with books all across the room, one closely behind the other, as far back as I could see. There were some spider webs among them, but the volumes did not seem to be damaged. Jimmie Gayle and Teebo pointed their flashlights at them with the circles of light playing on the titles. Dex let out a low whistle.

"They're all about voodoo and spells and ghosts—" Teebo's voice trailed off.

Jimmie Gayle took up the narration, "Look—legends of the south, black magic, hauntings, herbs—"

By this time I had been pushed into the room by onlookers trying to see. Oh, how I longed to be on Betty Mae's back porch with Dan reciting *Peyton Place*! The books were neatly lined up, and they were in alphabetical order. Someone had taken great care to organize them. Jimmie Gayle pulled one out.

"You'd better not do that," cautioned Dex.

"Why not—there's no one to ask permission," Jimmie Gayle said. He thumbed through the old pages. "Obviously this place has been sealed for ages." He was trying to see what was in the book. "All kinds of spells—the ingredients for potions—I don't believe it!" He looked in the front of the book. "*Property of Donald McQuaid.* Hey—I heard my dad talking about the McQuaids one time. They lived here until Donald disappeared. He was supposed to be into witchcraft or something. These must have been his."

"We'd better go," announced Trey.

"No, wait a minute," Jimmie Gayle said thoughtfully. "There's got to be some explanation." He turned a page. "This book is dated 1939. That's a long time after the Civil War. This wall you fell through was put up by the McQuaids, I'll bet. This space is just big enough to hold the books. Someone must have been trying to hide them—to keep anyone from getting *at* them."

"Or keep them—or something else *in*," Hally mused.

"Yeah," Claudia chimed in, "remember Pandora's Box—maybe we're letting an evil curse—or being—*out*! We'd better go!"

Several flashlights were searching the wall, the floor, the book titles.

"Why didn't they just throw them away? Why didn't they burn them?" Betty Mae inquired.

Jimmie Gayle looked at her as though she were out of her mind.

"Now, how should *I* know? I just got here myself." Several of us laughed nervously.

Claudia leaned over to whisper, "This is one time Patsy Kay is going to be sorry she's one of the Enlightened Baptists. Can you imagine what's it's going to be like when she hears about this and she missed it?!?!"

Teebo erupted with an evil chuckle. He had a couple of books in his hands, trying to balance the flashlight in order to read. I offered to hold the light, but I did not want to touch any of the books. It appeared that all of the books had belonged to Donald McQuaid. There was a bunch of papers among them, all bound together, with a date on the front, like that was the date they had been put away. September 30, 1940.

"Isn't that about the time Donald McQuaid disappeared?" asked Jimmie Gayle. I think that's about when my dad said—." He was obviously trying very hard to remember whatever details he could.

"The whole family moved away," said a voice behind. "Donald McQuaid was never found—not his dead body, nothing—just like Baxter Bridges."

Another voice inquired, "What are we going to do?"

"Tell Sheriff Brimley?"

"NO!!!" all other voices replied in unison.

"You're crazy if you think that stupid idiot would have a clue what to do," Dex mused. Teebo, Claudia, and I looked at each other. Dex ought to know.

"Let's keep this to ourselves," said Teebo. "When we see what's what, we can decide what to do. Maybe we can come out here in the daylight to see what's going on."

"We'll have to do it pretty quick," said Jimmie Gayle. "The books have been protected all this time by being sealed in here. Obviously the wall is decaying and letting in air, so we have to do something before it rains or somethin'. The season's over so we don't have football practice—we can come out tomorrow. You working at the cleaners tomorrow?"

Teebo replied he could get free. I knew he would be here with Jimmie Gayle regardless. Dex said he had plans. Out of his line of vision Claudia shot me a knowing look and mimed shoveling. Hally, Betty Mae, and I had band practice and Claudia said she would not be caught dead back out there.

"Don't say 'dead'," Teebo repeated.

We left it up to the boys, and we all swore ourselves to secrecy. We filed out of the small area where the books were and the guys looked around for something to hide the hole Trey had made when he fell. As we admired our handiwork, we were making sure we had everything done when Jimmie Gayle abruptly said, "Quiet, everybody!"

As hush fell over us as we looked at him. "What is it?" Teebo said.

"Will you be QUIET?!"

We were still. There seemed to be a rumble somewhere.

"The drums!" Dex exclaimed.

We all looked at each other, turned, and fairly flew across the stone floor toward the cars. Teebo helped the girls down, and we all rushed away from the house. As we kept going, Jimmie Gayle, who was in the lead and holding up the barbed wire while we slid through the fence, reminded, "Remember, mum's the word!"

We got to the cars to find a gathering of the others who had not gone to the house. They were dying to know what had gone on, but we just jumped in the cars and once again began to follow Jimmie Gayle's dust.

I don't know if Teebo called in sick or what, but the next afternoon he was not delivering dry cleaning. Jimmie Gayle had picked him up in a pickup he had gotten from his daddy's car lot and they had sped out to Beau Rivage to investigate our find. Hally and I hoped band practice would be over sooner than usual, but fat chance we had of that. Claudia had her mama's car that day and said she would go park over at The Quarter to do her daily quota of cigarettes (when she had her mama's car Claudia stood outside and leaned on the fender while puffing away), get the scoop from the guys when they returned, and then come pick us up from the band hall.

Although band practice went on forever as usual, Claudia picked us up saying the boys had not returned. It was already dark, but we went back to the Dam Road and waited at The Quarter after calling our folks that we were getting supper at Shug's. We did get some burgers and fries there but went back to await the guys. We had to sit about an hour before they whizzed past us, and Claudia blew the horn as we followed trying to get them to stop.

"Look—they've got a tarp tied down with stuff under it," Claudia observed.

"Oh, no!" exclaimed Hally, "don't tell me they lifted some of that stuff in the hole! Suppose it's cursed or something!"

Jimmie Gayle's arm could be seen outside the driver's window pointing in the direction of Shug's, so we followed to the drive-in before he stopped. Then he and Teebo jumped out of the pickup and collapsed on our back seat.

"Home again, home again, jiggity jog," Teebo gasped.

They were covered with dust and were obviously exhausted. The carhop came over and got their order of burgers, fries, and emergency cokes, and the two boys began to describe their afternoon.

They had gone straight out, parked as close to the ruins as possible, and taken boxes and shovels with them. Jimmie Gayle had taken the precaution of taking his hunting rifle, although Teebo had pointed out it probably would do no good against any haunting entities that might try to spook them. They had re-opened the hole and taken some lanterns since darkness was descending early. They had pulled out some books and looked through them. They were indeed about casting spells, histories of hauntings, ghost stories, legends from everywhere that had anything to do with occult practices. All were in alphabetical/chronological order. They decided to pack them up and get them out of the weather. Jimmie Gayle's family had an obscure shed at the back of some property they owned at the city limits. The shed was rarely opened, and Jimmie Gayle felt the books could be stored there until further plans were made. The boys had loaded up the back of the pickup and still had books left to gather, so they sealed the hole once more and had come on back. They had heard no drums and nothing out of the ordinary had occurred.

"Hey, didn't John August go out there once and something happened?" recalled Teebo.

"He won't talk about it," I said. "Whatever it was must have been horrible. You remember he was out of school for a long time about two years ago. It was when Baxter Bridges disappeared."

"We've got to talk to him," Jimmie Gayle said resolutely. "Maybe if he knew we'd heard drums—someone said *he* heard them."

"Yeah," Hally recalled, "and a lot of people wouldn't believe him. Wouldn't believe much of anything he said. But Bax did go back out to Beau Rivage and he never came back—that made believers out of some people."

"I think maybe we'd better leave John out of this," I said, "—he'd probably like to forget about it. This will just dredge everything up and upset him again."

"Yeah," responded Hally. "Let's do what we can without bothering him."

"But if he knew I'd heard the drums—and then *y'all* had—" Jimmie Gayle mused, "it might help him to know he's not in this by himself."

"I think he took himself *out* of it a long time ago. Why don't we wait and see what we can find out first," Teebo suggested. "If we can solve anything, then maybe we can help him. If we think it might hurt him more, we can spare him."

It crossed my mind for the umpteenth time that I really had some wonderful friends. They were really good people.

We all agreed and decided since it probably would not rain before the end of the school week, we could go out to Beau Rivage on Saturday—in the daylight, of course—and get the rest of the books. The guys, more brave and curious, wanted to go through them, a project that could be conducted without deadline in the shed. Teebo resolved to call in sick again on Saturday—his mama was going over to the University and he could stage one of his miraculous recoveries, help with the project, help with the books, and be back in bed with a relapse by the time she got home. Hally and I could always say we had to practice twirling, and for that to take all day was nothing unusual. Claudia frequently studied with me, so we were all covered for the task at hand.

Saturday, although my mother was surprised that I rose so early, she knew what dedicated band members we all were, and I departed "for Hally's." This would be speeded up considerably by Jimmie Gayle's meeting me a block away to take me there, where we got Hally and met Claudia, who was driving her daddy's pickup with Teebo at her side. We caravanned it to Beau Rivage and spent all day loading the books, taking them back to Jimmie Gayle's shed, unloading our cargo and going back for another load. I wore gloves—I guess I felt if I did not actually *touch* the books, maybe no spell would be cast on me—I don't know. Anyway, we were totally spent by the time we had placed all the boxes in the shed. It had been a long day, and we had learned a little about the books as we worked, not being able to resist the temptation to thumb through as we went. It seemed the most valuable find might be a diary that Donald McQuaid had kept, which Jimmie Gayle decided to sneak home. We warned him that that might be a bad move, but Jimmie Gayle was not afraid of anything and pointed out that he, too, was a Presbyterian.

It was almost dark when we locked the shed for the last time. We were relieved and tired, and Jimmie Gayle had a date with Sallybeth for which he did not want to be late. We said our goodbyes and the two pickups started back up the dirt road across the property which led to the paved street beyond. As we turned on to the pavement, a storm abruptly broke. Just like that. It had been a beautiful, sunny day with no hint of rain until right before the storm hit. The rain, as sudden as it was, came down in torrents and the windshield wipers could not keep visible the path before us. Lightning flashed in forks across the sky and a deafening crash of thunder rolled. I looked back through the rear window of the pickup and saw an unbelievable sight in the distance—a brilliant bolt of lightning struck the shed, and we instantly heard another clap of thunder that seemed to engulf us—it was more powerful than the first and terribly frightening.

"Jimmie Gayle!" I screamed. "The shed's on fire!"

"What??!!" Jimmie Gayle gasped, looking around.

Sure enough, we could see that the smoking shed had burst into flames. Jimmie Gayle wheeled the pickup around through the grass and back onto the road as we headed back to the little building, now totally ablaze.

"I can't believe it—we just left it!" he said, careening the pickup around the turn and thrusting it over the ground.

"Don't go back there," Hally cautioned, "Let's get out of here! Time to rock an' *roll!*"

"Time to cut bait," I agreed.

Jimmie Gayle was not to be deterred. We were being followed by Claudia and Teebo, and the pair of trucks screeched to a halt just short of the shed. Despite the pounding torrent of rain, the shed was almost gone. It seemed that only seconds had passed since I had seen the lightning strike the building. We debated whether to get out and try to salvage some of the books, but no one wanted to press our luck. We watched the flames consume the whole sight before us and die quickly in the rain. The entire event had taken just a few minutes.

"Well, I'm glad I've still got the diary," Jimmie Gayle said thoughtfully.

"Jimmie Gayle," Hally warned, "you better throw that thing right into the whole mess over there—quick, before the fire is all out! This can't be coincidence."

"Yes it can. I don't believe this was anything but a normal happening. Was Claudia smoking in there?"

"No," I answered. "The only time she lit up, she came outside and sat in the truck—I'm allergic to the smoke so she always tries to keep it away from me."

"Yeah, that's right," he remembered. "She does try to do that for you."

"Jimmie Gayle," Hally began again, "pleeeeese throw that book away. *Now!*"

Teebo was standing in the storm beating on the window.

"Hey, Man," he said to Jimmie Gayle, "you'd better throw that book in there. Give it to me. I'll do it. And *LET'S GET OUT OF HERE!*"

Jimmie Gayle was resolute. "No. Not before I read it."

He told Teebo we would leave, however, and we started back to civilization. Jimmie Gayle said he wanted to go back to Beau Rivage to see if anything happened out there. Hally and I did not want to go, having had our fill of strange occurrences for one day.

"Jimmie Gayle," I said, "you don't want to be late for your date. You know how Sallybeth's mama is. You just go on and we'll see you tomorrow. We can all go tomorrow afternoon. I'll call Teebo and Claudia. Everybody'll think we're going to the picture show, but we'll just go to Beau Rivage. And there is something to be said for daylight."

"And the Sabbath Day," reminded Hally.

Jimmie Gayle agreed, and we all started home—tired, scared, dirty, and relieved. But just as we got a block from Shug's, Jimmie Gayle made one of his death-defying U turns and headed for The Quarter. I knew what *that* meant and so did Hally. We also knew it meant to keep our mouths entirely shut. We hung on for dear life as we were all pressed against the passenger-side door during the turn and then sped out to the Dam Road. I was grateful to see Claudia's pickup behind us. She and Teebo—what friends! I knew they did not want to go either. We got to the turn-off to

Beau Rivage in record time and never slowed down as we bumped and swerved in the twilight. The headlights of the truck danced along the gravel we passed over, its red clay having provided a pathway for missions of all kinds over the last centuries. The Chickasaws, the Choctaws, hunters, the soldiers of foreign countries as well as our own, whether serving the United States or the Confederacy. As I hung on bracing myself from flying all over the pickup cab I knew no one had ever gone over this road for the reason we were on it.

"Leave it to us," I thought, "no noble cause to die for—we're not going to get shot trying to deliver a message that would save hundreds of lives. We'll probably just die of fright." I knew if we did see any ghosts, if we died, if the curse of Beau Rivage struck us down, no one would ever know. People around town would just say we crazy teenagers had done some fool thing and gotten ourselves killed. Well, they would be right about *that*! This was about the dumbest thing we had ever done. But Jimmie Gayle was a man possessed. And there was no question that we would never let him go out to Beau Rivage tonight alone.

We left the gravel and turned onto the dirt road. The dirt was damp, but as we neared Beau Rivage it became mud and slush. Finally we were once again at Beau Rivage Castle. Jimmie Gayle hit the breaks, which practically threw Hally and me against the dashboard, and Claudia just missed rear-ending us. Jimmie Gayle darted out of the truck and made for the ruins, vaulting the barbed wire like a gazelle. We were running behind his obsessed stride, twigs and briars reaching out for us and scratching and snagging us with every step. Then we saw the smoke. We all broke into a run. The crumbling walls of Beau Rivage loomed before us. The walls that may have seen brilliant parties on soft summer nights and cold Christmases. The walls that likely had seen the Yankees storm through the South. The walls that knew The Secret.

We saw that lightning had struck a tree right on the other side of the secret room's outside wall and the top of the tree lay across it. We got to the porch and climbed up. The hole was open, burned around the edges. We looked into the smoldering darkness to see that the rest of the tree, embers still red, had crashed through the ceiling. Everything in the room was burned to a crisp.

Without our secret to discuss, for a while the best the town could do for gossip was discuss Madeleine Vander Meer's lawsuit against Spike Trammel, the recount of which was taking up a great deal of space in the weekly *Addisonian*. Madeleine was suing Spike because his dog had bitten her while she was jogging in his neighborhood trying to catch J. T. Roberson's attention. Madeleine lived across town but drove over to Rolling Hills to jog, since J. T. Roberson had kept his house in his divorce settlement and she thought she would enjoy living in it just fine. Spike's dog was eating out in his yard when she loped by (Madeleine was never known any more for her coordination than common sense) and stopped to pet him. Apparently the dog thought she was after his supper—or that she was part of it, because he jumped up and bit her. Since Spike happened to be the local judge, Madeleine no doubt thought she could get some fine-looking jogging outfits at Goldsmith's after a settlement so as to look her best when J. T. looked out his window during her subsequent jogs. The documentation on this litigation took up space on the front page for several weeks—right up until one Sunday night when a loud bang was heard and a dead body was found in a car right in front of the sheriff's office.

Vernon Kent had just moved to town to help run the local office of Regional Gas Transmission. He had with him his perky blond wife Beverly, soon labeled a total ditz. Vernon was very quiet and did not join the Rotary or the Lions Club, but when they joined the country club it was soon known he was the best golfer in town. He had to go out of town quite a bit, and one time during one of his absences, Beverly got a speeding ticket on the interstate en route to Memphis. Pretty soon it got around town via Battle in one generation and Patsy Kay in ours, that there was a state trooper's car at her house every night thereafter until Vernon came back home. This began to be a routine—Vernon would depart on his trip, and the trooper would arrive on his. The Waltrips lived across the street, and Sallybeth said he would park his motorcycle down the block, but it made so much noise when he rode up that everybody on the street knew what was what. Something like this just did not go on in Addison. But here we had an officer of the law not subject to election turnover, not raised in the community and therefore unafraid of the Enlightened Ladies who through self appointment policed the local morals. There did not seem to be anything they could do but discuss it at prayer meeting and over cooling glasses of lemonade. Beverly finally decided to leave Vernon (there were no divorced couples within the city limits, so this was a huge step for her to take) and thought she would take him to the cleaners in the process. After she moved into an apartment in the same house on Chestnut Street where the aforementioned state trooper had his, Patsy Kay immediately went over to befriend the friendless Beverly (none of the Enlightened Ladies would have a thing to do with her, even at church) and get all the scoop. According to Patsy Kay, Beverly determined that whatever process by which she was going to clean Vernon's clock was the wrong one—apparently with her abandonment and no children, Vernon was not going to have to shell out to the extent she had expected. For background, Patsy Kay additionally reported Beverly and Vernon had been married only two years before, after Beverly had started granting the already-married Vernon favors beyond his wildest dreams after their days of work at the gas company in Nashville. She had finally given the infatuated Vernon, who was by now addicted to her physical therapy, an ultimatum and he had left his alcoholic wife and two children and made an honest woman out of Beverly. Honest but not too bright.

Faced with having to get a job, the panic-stricken Beverly tried to make up with Vernon, who would have none of her—so when he went out of town the next time, Beverly moved back into their house (Vernon, for all his *business* acumen, had not had the good *sense* to change the locks or file any papers). Ditsy Beverly *did* have the locks changed (I could at least see the state trooper behind this—if Vernon would not think of it, Beverly *never* would) and *she* then sued *Vernon* for abandonment. To top that off, she achieved further celebrity when she had a burglar alarm put in, the first residential alarm in town. People began to wonder what sort of valuables she had in there. When Vernon got back home, she would not even let him in to get his clothes and he had to go over to Chimes' Men's Wear and get all outfitted for our early, very unexpected cold snap.

The state trooper, whose name was Harvey, drove a car while on duty, but he would have made a good motorcycle cop. He tinkered with a couple of motorcycles around the house on Chestnut Street, and they were quite obviously his pride and joy. He even rented extra space in Mr. Garrett's garage so he could keep them there at night and protected from the weather.

That winter on a particularly cold Saturday afternoon, Harvey decided to work on one of his motorcycles. There being no heat in the garage, he decided to work on it in his kitchen. He could not get it up the steps to his first-floor apartment, so he got a couple of two-by-fours so he could ride the motorcycle up onto the porch and take it inside. This seemed good in theory, but in practice, he gunned the powerful machine just a tad too hard and it went crashing right through his front door into the living room. He was lying there moaning and groaning when Beverly walked in, and she called the sheriff's office for someone to take the trooper to the doctor's office, as it appeared he had broken his leg. Talbert Dinkins, who had been pursuing a career in local law enforcement since he committed the grave error of letting Zella enter the governor's mansion unannounced, was glad to oblige.

Harvey had indeed broken his leg, and Dr. Butz put a big cast on it. Talbert then took Harvey back home, where Beverly was trying to clean up the mess and close the gaping hole in the front of Harvey's apartment. She saw the squad car drive up, and ran to the bathroom to wash her hands. Unable to get the grease off, she saw some turpentine and wiped it on her hands with some toilet paper, disposing of the toilet paper in the commode. She then ran out to help Talbert bring Harvey inside the house.

Harvey was deposited on the sofa and Talbert went back to the sheriff's office. Harvey was still moaning and groaning, but he was mainly just disgusted with the whole turn of events.

"Hon, get me a beer while I go to the john, will you?" he directed Beverly.

"Sure you don't need help getting down the hall?" the solicitous Beverly inquired.

"No, just the beer." By this time Harvey had made it to the bathroom, despite holding a cigarette between fingers that were trying to also hold the crutches, and closed the door. He had not seen the turpentine on the sink and when he whirled the crutches around, the turpentine fell into the john. As he was lunging to catch it, the cigarette also fell into the toilet. Beverly was opening the refrigerator door when the explosion blew out the bathroom wall.

She ran in to Harvey, who was writhing on the floor, moaning and groaning again and holding his other leg. A crowd was gathering where the wall used to be and Beverly hollered for somebody to call the sheriff's office. Talbert Dinkins arrived johnny-on-the-spot once more, and when he heard what happened, he laughed so hard he was still laughing while trying to get Harvey into the patrol car. He fell back on Harvey, who hit the ground just so and broke his wrist. On the way to the doctor's office yet again, when he came to the stop sign by The Old Draper House, Talbert glanced in the back seat to see about Harvey. Seeing the miserable Harvey's face just set Talbert off again and when his foot accidentally hit the accelerator, he roared into Johnnie Kat who was backing her car out of her driveway.

Harvey was catapulted from the back seat, over the dashboard, through the windshield, and after bouncing onto the hood of the car, he landed in the street where the astonished Miss Thelma Swango hit him with her car. Miss Thelma hurriedly backed up in order to get off Harvey and hit a telephone pole which crashed onto a fire hydrant that erupted into a terrific geyser, drenching the dazed Harvey lying on the pavement. But it did bring him to.

The town was alerted when the signal went off for the volunteer fire department, as the siren was so loud it could be heard for miles around the city limits. The new red fire truck arrived clanging away and fire fighters, scattered all over town and environs at their respective jobs, appeared straightaway, along with the curious, for the emergency. The editor of *The Addisonian* ran over with his new Polaroid. This was the most electrifying moment in Addison since Lena Sue's daddy's last night on earth.

Brother Fox from the Enlightened Morning Star Baptist Church was coming out of the house next door and was certain he had just seen a miracle since when Harvey landed he was not hurt any more than he already was when he got into the ill-fated car. He made a clean sail through the windshield, and Miss Thelma always drove at a slow poke, so she was hardly moving when Harvey hit the pavement in front of her. As Brother Fox bent over Harvey on the street, telling him all this was a warning to repent, he converted Harvey right there on the scene as the geyser rained down upon them. Teebo said he personally thought the whole production rivaled Charlton Heston's parting of the Red Sea.

Martha Louise Potter called the emergency bridge party for the next afternoon, and it was agreed by the Enlightened Ladies while Teresa Hooper, Billy's mama, made her four clubs that after all the scandal with Beverly, Harvey was merely getting his come-uppance. By the time Beverly tried to divorce Vernon, who used all of this material in court, when he was through she was lucky she didn't have to pay *him*.

In the spring NASA introduced seven Mercury Astronauts. They were going into outer space. They were going to orbit the earth. They were going to land on the moon! We had seen Captain Video and Buck Rogers at the picture show when we were little children and then gone home and played space ship on the huge tree Battle had cut down in our back yard. Terry and I installed bent coathangers and other sculptured wire at a chopped-out point up the trunk and had a grand cockpit. But these men were going to do it for real! April 9, 1959.

Not long after that, we all met at the phone booth one Sunday night and Teebo decided *he* would lead the pack. Trey, Claudia, Hally, and I were in his car as we made the customary rounds about town to see if anything of interest was stirring. As usual nothing was. After looping Shug's we were duty bound to hit the dam and do the levee bit, so away we went.

The moon was especially bright, and as we sped across the levee, I looked out over the water. Its reflection in the waves made the large reservoir look as if it were sprinkled with dancing stars. We made the run through the picnic areas—still and cool in the night breeze—and around spillway—with its deafening roar of gushing water—without incident, and I was relieved Teebo was leading, for I knew the last thing he would do was turn off to Beau Rivage. We headed back to town, all knowing we would just end up on Betty Mae's back porch as usual. Dan Crockett had graduated to reciting *Lady Chatterley's Lover*.

When we got back to the square, everything was quite, and most folks except the Baptists (who were still holding forth) had gone home after Sunday night church. We cruised the loop which made up Humphrey Place, mainly to see if Patsy Kay were living with Biff that week—they seemed to break up every other weekend and she would move back home until the following Sunday night. They would break up on a Friday, Sonny would send some workers and a van over to move her out, furniture and all. Then the next Friday Biff would go say he was sorry and the van would go back to Humphrey Place and the workers would move Patsy Kay back in.

We were about to parade through the town square again when the sudden sound of a gunshot brought us to a halt.

"Must be a car backfiring," Teebo decreed.

"Maybe not," cautioned Hally.

Jimmie Gayle's car turned in the direction of the sound, and Teebo wheeled around to follow.

"Suppose it's *not* a backfire?" I inquired, hoping Teebo would think better of following the devil-may-care Jimmie Gayle into a hail of bullets. After all, everyone would look to Teebo for the decision since he was leading the pack that night.

"Then we can't leave him by himself," replied the ever-loyal Teebo as he made the U turn and put a heavy foot on the gas to catch Jimmie Gayle. I might have known.

"Yeah," said Claudia taking a puff, "after we're killed together we can just have a mass burial. I hear the funeral home quit giving out happy face calendars. This year it's fly swatters."

After Beau Rivage, we sort of took it for granted one day Addison would be devoid of our whole class, even the Presbyterians.

At least Trey was also in the car. We passed the sheriff's office, from whence the sound had come, as it brought the sleepy deputies running out the door and down the steps to the Cadillac out front, which still had its motor running. When the door was opened by Talbert Dinkins, Ace Deputy, the head of a lifeless body fell on Talbert's high-sheen boots. The shocked Deputy Dinkins immediately cordoned off the area and we were told to keep moving, so we never saw anything but the car. But with 15 carloads of us in attendance and dispersing like buckshot, word spread quickly and lights began to go on all over town.

"Wonder who it is?" Hally said when Teebo returned to the car to tell what had occurred, but with no names.

"Prob'ly Harvey—Vernon Kent musta caught up with 'im," joked Teebo.

People began to arrive on the scene in pajama tops and bedroom slippers, though none of the ladies arrived with their hair still in curlers, as this would have been unseemly. Teebo saw his daddy talking to Talbert and said, "S'cuse me—Mr. Justice, please see to the ladies. I must needs acquire the information."

He slid out of the car and vanished in the sea of men gathered at the front of the sheriff's office.

"What new earth-shaking event will happen next!" Hally exclaimed.

"You think this shooting is earth shaking?" inquired Trey.

"No! I mean Teebo's been paying attention in English class!" laughed Hally.

We exploded in giggles riddled with anxiety. Teebo seemed gone a long time, but actually returned in a few minutes with the name of the person shot. Was it Vernon or was it Harvey? We were stunned when he said, "Jerry Meadows."

No one had seen or heard of Jerry since he and Becky had left town. Her parents always had kept to themselves anyway, and after the peeping-tom incident Mrs. Smith never went out even to the grocery store. All Sullivan's deliveries were left on the back porch and Mrs. Smith would send Junior a check for the food. Calvin was a carpenter and never socialized or participated in civic activities, so neither parent was ever really available to ask how the Meadows were doing—but it was evident that night that at least Jerry was not doing well. Talbert had called Dr. Butz at home and Sheriff Brimley. Brimley then called Calvin, who said that he did not even know that Jerry was in town. He said as far as he knew, Becky was still in Kentucky.

It seems there was nothing to indicate foul play—in fact, there was a suicide note and a copy of Jerry's will on the front seat. Although the note said he was sorry to end things this way, and the handwriting seemed to match that in some other papers in the car, Jerry gave no reason for his final, very public act.

Elvis came home to his country and home to Graceland in March of 1960.

That summer Teebo and Terry decided to be Tom Sawyer and Huckleberry Finn. They built a raft on the banks of the Tallahatchie River, loaded it with supplies, and shoved off with the gang on the riverbank waving good-bye. The boys' parents checked on them from the air, as by that time Sallybeth's daddy had a small airplane, and once a week one of the parents would, in turn, go up with Mr. Waltrip and follow the progress the adventurers were making. They knew the boys were responsible, but they also knew Teebo could not swim. Although Terry was pretty much a fish, the parents also knew if the boys got in trouble in the water, that Terry would never leave Teebo. The guys floated safely way past Greenwood into the Yazoo and came back all suntanned and muscular. After their return Teebo wrote four articles for publication in *The Addisonian* about their odyssey.

In December of our senior year we were still all heady about being the state football champions. Everyone was still in a celebratory mood, and in December it was decided "A Christmas Carol" would be presented the last day before the holidays. Teebo was to play Scrooge, and I was the Christmas Fairy who was to show him the past, present, and future. We all really worked hard on the production. Learning lines, rehearsing until late at night, decorating the stage, making costumes. The day before the play Teebo came down with the mumps. The cast and crew and band members that made up the orchestra were called to a special meeting in the auditorium just before our first classes. Miss Whitley was hysterical—you would have thought the Russians were fixing to bomb us all to kingdom come.

"What will we do? What *will* we do?" She whirled stage left. "We'll just have to cancel the play! If we had a few days, we could let someone read the lines—everyone would understand." She whirled stage right. "But there's no time to practice! We have to *cancel*!"

Jay had been working the stage lights during our rehearsals, and when she started wringing her hands and wailing and carrying on, he stepped onto the stage and said quietly, "I'll be Scrooge." Just like that. Miss Whitley was so shocked, she actually was struck speechless. But not for long.

She then turned to Miss Greenway and said so we all could hear, "He's a *football player*, for heaven sake! How on earth can a *football player* learn to read those lines? Certainly not overnight! He wouldn't be able to *read* dramatically. He even failed a grade!"

That made me mad. Jay had *missed* a grade with rheumatic fever! She knew that. I was sitting on the front row and stood up. "He didn't fail a grade—he was sick. He can do it! I *know* he can! I'll help him. Just about everything he has to say, he has to say to me. And I know his sisters'll help him tonight. He's been here for every rehearsal. Give him a chance!"

Everyone was pretty much thunderstruck I had said anything. I made straight A's in Miss Whitley's class. I was one of her little intellectual darlings. My mama taught school now—I never made any waves. I must be nuts to risk my A. But they also knew Jay was a very special friend of mine. They knew that put a whole different slant on things.

All the other kids started saying, "Yeah" and "Give him a chance" and "Whydontcha." I guess they figured if *I'*d speak up, what the hell. They started standing up and waving their arms and saying "Yeah" some more. I think Miss Whitley feared a rumble. She gave a heaving sigh and the way she gave Jay the play book was a gesture like throwing down a gauntlet. I thought she was going to slam it down on the floor at his feet. She all but *dared* Jay to read the lines well. She glared at him, "Do what you can."

I spent lunch and study hall with Jay and then met him after band practice at Shug's. We ate burgers and rehearsed surrounded by a downright reverent silence—sort of like church. No one played the juke box. No one spoke to us. There was nothing to break our concentration. I was sure someone was seeing how we were doing then went somewhere else to report to the gang. Jay took me home about ten o'clock. Betty Lou was a nurse in town now and she and Jamie Ann were waiting his arrival with coffee and determination.

The next day we all gathered behind the stage for the curtain to go up. Miss Whitley had not even spoken to Jay, who was sitting alone in a corner studying the play book. I walked over to him. He looked up.

"You are going to be a wonderful Scrooge!" I declared.

He smiled. "I'll try. Betty Lou and Jamie Ann stayed up all night with me. They even put my costume together."

"Did you get any sleep?" I asked, not surprised at their efforts.

"No—but I can sleep tonight."

"Don't worry about anything. I'm right there beside you the whole time," I said, hoping I was being reassuring.

The Spirit of Christmas Past, otherwise known as Hally Jordan, walked up about that time, brightly announcing, "Miss Whitley said to tell you to get on stage, Jay. The curtain is about to go up. Good luck! We're all behind you!"

Jay stood up. He was a lot taller than we were, but he stood especially straight and looked a lot taller that day. He took a deep breath, put his play book down, and said, "Okay. Thanks."

He walked toward the stage.

"Jay!" I called, "you forgot your play book!" I picked it up and ran to him.

He shook his head and smiled as he waved me off, "I didn't forget it." He walked onstage.

The curtain went up. He was on the stage alone. Everyone had heard what was going on with Miss Whitley, and when the stage lights went on, applause broke out in the audience. All of us backstage joined in. Miss Whitley peered out into the audience from behind the curtain and looked very disgusted. I figured she was seeing who was applauding so she could give out F's.

Jay had the first lines and spoke them clearly and with authority. He got up and walked around while he spoke. He leaned nonchalantly with his elbow on the fireplace mantle, reciting with expression and confidence. He seemed as though he were in his own home, lord of the manor. And he did not have his play book.

Hally and I were watching from the wings.

"Heavens!" Hally gasped. "He learned the lines! He learned *all those lines*!"

"He surely did," I grinned. I was so proud of him!

"But it's just the first of the play," she cautioned.

"Don't worry," I assured her. "He's got them down. He wouldn't be out there without the book if he needed it. He stepped forward just to help us out so we wouldn't have to cancel the play. He knew how hard we'd all been working on it. But Miss Whitley made a big mistake to try to embarrass him for it. She's going to be humiliated. She's going down!" I could feel it in the air.

"I hope so," Hally said wistfully.

Soon it was my cue. I appeared to the startled Scrooge and began to show him his evil past. Hally emerged from the wings to tell him all about it. He turned to watch and I gave him a discreet pat on the back. He looked back a second and winked. He was so at ease you would have thought he were on the football field or the basketball court. Then came Christmas Present and Christmas Future. Then the visit to the Cratchits and "God bless us every one!" The curtain came down. Jay had given the whole performance on one day's notice and had not fluffed a single line.

What Enid Whitley had not counted on was Jay was doing this for *us*. And he was a star athlete who lettered in four sports to whom she had issued the challenge. He was dedicated. He could focus. He could prepare. When we were at Shug's there was nothing else on this planet for him but me and the play book. He had gotten ready for this with the same intensity he had gotten ready for the State Championship game. The very thing Whitley had put him down for was his strength—he was a champion.

The curtain calls began. The Cratchits; the Christmases—Past, Present and Future; me; then Jay. When he walked onto the stage, the audience went wild. He got a thunderous standing ovation! The whole school erupted. Then someone shouted, "God bless *Jay*, every one!" Then a cheer! The whole school started chanting, "Jay! Jay! Jay!"

Jay looked surprised. He looked down at me. I gave him a great, big hug. As I did, he whispered, "I can't believe this. Is all this really going on?"

I laughed and said, "You bet it is!" You not only saved the day, you saved the play! You've proved that you can be a hero in something besides sports!"

He laughed and then looked back into the audience, still chanting his name. Then everyone on stage gathered around him to congratulate him. Trey and Jimmie Gayle ran up the aisle and vaulted onto the stage. As they brushed past me, Trey whispered, "I think we're about to fail English!"

With that, he and Jimmie Gayle hoisted Jay to their shoulders and started carrying him around the set. The cast all fell in line behind the boys and the small band convened for the production raised their horns. Andy Brumfield stood up, took a stance that would have thrilled ol' Tacawaw to pieces, and his trumpet began to blare "When the Saints Go Marching In." The whole school was clapping in time—even the teachers. Even Malcolm P. Clovis! The whole school except for one. The mortified, humbled Miss Whitley was nowhere to be seen. Someone said they had just seen her running in tears toward the teacher's lounge. That was the last year she taught at Addison High School. Before she left the school that day for the holiday vacation, she told ol' Malcolm P. that she would be retiring at the end of the year.

After starring in football and "A Christmas Carol," when the holidays were over, Jay continued his stellar performance on the basketball court. We were sure the team would be as good this year as the football team had been. One day, though, right before the regional tournament, Jay got sick. He was taken off the court with a horrible pain in his head. He had trouble with his vision and his heart was racing. The coach was very concerned about him and called his mama, and when she took him to the doctor, Jay was rushed to a hospital in Memphis for fear his rheumatic fever had indeed severely damaged his heart—or something worse had happened. His sister Betty had arranged for the best doctors available to examine him. Rumors swirled. We wondered if he would have to have a heart operation. Someone was talking about a brain tumor. Although with Jay playing we had expected to take the whole tournament with no trouble at all, no one really cared about the tournament anymore. At noon on Friday, we just wanted Jay to be okay. The cafeteria was strangely quiet. No clanging of silverware, no crashing plates. No one was eating very much. We were all waiting word from Jay's mama, who had promised to call the principal as soon as there was word. That was all we talked about, and I was saying silent prayers all day. In fact Sallybeth, who read the devotional over the P.A. system that morning, had led a special prayer for Jay before classes began. About two o'clock, we heard the static on the p.a. system that always preceded the booming voice of Malcolm P. Clovis.

"May I have your attention, please. Mrs. Brent just called and said she would take Jay directly to the tournament. He'll meet the team there." Malcolm P. had not interrupted classes for anything but administrative matters since Patsy Kay had run off to Georgia.

A mighty cheer went up from every classroom in the high school building. It was better than anything ever hollered at any pep rally. Greater than Scrooge's standing ovation. It could be heard a block away. There was no damage to Jay's heart; he had been diagnosed with migraine headaches. He was going to be fine! In the midst of all the cheering I saw heads bowed and tearful eyes on smiling faces.

Jay went on to star in college football, basketball, baseball, and track, and ended up coaching over in the delta—the *"football player"* was teaching in college! He married the girl of his dreams. I had always known how he loved Sallybeth, but I was sworn to secrecy. Time did tell. They lived happily ever after while Jay was also faculty sponsor of the Drama Club.

Our days of marching were almost over. Finally the band boarded the schoolbuses for the State Band Contest. Nothing would do but the triple crown. No Addison band had ever achieved the triple crown—superiors in concert, sight reading, and marching. We had taken a vow and just about killed ourselves practicing for the last three months. All those hours and days and weeks and months of marching. The sweat. The aching muscles. The blisters. One day at the football field Hally showed up with a temperature of 100 degrees. As drum majorette, she did not want to let anyone down. Playing "Die Meistersinger"—Andy Brumfield was calling it "Damn Meistersinger" long before we left that early morning for the state capital. But we took State Contest by storm! We would not be denied. We won the Triple Crown.

The day after as the band was driven in two school buses from the state capital, when we were about 15 miles from Addison we looked up with alarm to see a string of cars on the side of the highway. The line stretched as far as we could see.

"Must be a pretty bad wreck," Hally said excitedly. "Look—there are flashing lights from a bunch of highway patrol cars." But there was no barrier to our passage, no patrolmen out on the highway diverting us or trying to get us to slow down. They were in their cars, one of which slid in front of us as it started up its siren and proceeded toward Addison. We assumed it was going to get us through the wreck ahead.

We started passing the cars parked on the side of the highway.

"Hey, that's Jimmie Gayle's mama in that car—and Mrs. Waltrip!" hollered Andy Brumfield as he pointed to the line of cars.

"There's Trey with Dan Crockett!" yelled Charles William Redwing. "And Mr. and Mrs. Seaton. And the Draper sisters."

"My God!" exclaimed Sallybeth. "There's Miss Thelma Swango!"

Horns started blowing. The people inside the cars were waving and we were hollering and waving back like crazy. We kept passing cars. Brimming schoolbuses. Claudia in the smokey cab of her daddy's pickup with Sarah Jane. Jimmie Gayle and Dex. Terry and Teebo. Betty Mae and Johnnie Kat. The cars were parked up the hill and down the next one. Patsy Kay and Biff. Mr. and Mrs. Throckmorton. Sonny and Hortense three cars up. Commercial vehicles. Robert Sample in his tv repair truck. My mother was in the car with Hally's parents. The lights flashing ahead were joined by the loud scream of sirens. In the distance, another siren. We reached to top of the hill. We still could not see the end of the cars parked ahead of us. Letitia and Bonnie had piled the cheerleaders in a convertible they had borrowed from Jimmie Gayle's daddy. Football season was long over, but they had dug out their uniforms and were belting out cheers they had made up just for us. We kept rolling past. The entire town of Addison, young and old, had turned out to welcome us. Obviously the town square had closed down—there could not have been anyone left to mind the stores. School had been dismissed early, and the country children who rode schoolbuses were driven to the celebration to join the parade before being driven home. Everything was done to make it possible for everyone to participate. Above the din we heard an airplane right overhead. We looked up to see Sallybeth's daddy flying his plane over the line on the highway, a sign trailing behind in the sky which read, "Addison Has A Superior Band." When Sallybeth saw it she burst into tears. We finally got to the head of the line and there sat the brand new fire truck which Mary Louise Potter had suffocated with crepe paper. Signs on it read, "Addison Band #1" and "All Superiors." Sheriff Buford Brimley was right behind, lights and siren going full force—his last official act, as he lost the election.

We knew people watched at football half-times and lined the street when we paraded, but we really did not know anyone but our parents had noticed how hard we were working to get ready for State Contest. When we were parading it was to celebrate for someone else—the football team. The homecoming queen. Santa Claus. Now the whole town had turned out to honor us! There wasn't a dry eye anywhere. We were totally overwhelmed. Overjoyed! This welcome had been put together in a matter of hours—we had just gotten our ratings the night before. When the football team had come back in the middle of the night right after winning the state championship, we had given the team a rousing celebration at school and in the town square. The band had played for them and paraded them around town. Now they were turned out for *us*! No one had ever gotten a reception such as the Addison High School Band got that day! What a memory to take to graduation!

* * *

The King was in his castle. Right before we graduated, Elvis went to Hawaii to give a concert which raised over $62,000 to finance the memorial to the U.S.S. Arizona. I never heard the evangelists say a word about it. When he returned to Hawaii several years later for another concert, that night he would be seen by more people than any entertainer in the history of the world—a billion people in 36 countries.

He would always be The King. He cast a long shadow.

Preparations for our high school graduation began about a month before school was out. We all learned the class song and the various crepe paper committees were appointed. The band practiced "Pomp and Circumstance"—everything was in readiness.

But one day graduation was the last thing on our minds. We reported to our home rooms and answered roll call. We had the Pledge to the Flag and the Lord's Prayer. After the morning devotional over the P.A. system, the voice of Malcolm P. Clovis was heard telling us to remain in place when the bell rang. Something more important than the next class was about to take place.

It was May 5, 1961. Alan Shepard was on top of a rocket on a launching pad down in Florida. We could hear mission control during the countdown. I said a prayer for him and looked around the room to see heads bowed and silent lips moving. Our prayers would go up with Alan Shepard in the rocket. We heard the blast-off. We heard "A-OK!" and "What a beautiful view!" But it wasn't over—we had to get him down safely. He flew outside our atmosphere and the capsule had to re-enter with the heat shield down just so. It turned just right. He was falling back to earth. I felt part of One America focused on our brave astronaut. I felt so close to the classmates sharing this historic moment with me—I would remember those minutes with them for the rest of my life. The first American in space! Alan Shepard splashed down to earth a hero, alive, well, and flashing that wonderful smile with all those teeth!

No one was particularly impressed that my cousin Bobby came down from Memphis to my graduation and took pictures. But everyone all over town was *very* impressed when the pictures were delivered with the signature in the bottom corner of the finest photographer in the South—Robert E. Hall of Memphis!

As we received our high school diplomas, pictures of a different kind flashed through my mind. It had been an eventful year. For such a little town, Addison's youngsters had performed remarkably. After we were the state football champions and the band got its superiors, our basketball team had won the conference title. Maybe there was something to that artesian water thing after all. Trey was getting a grant-in-aid to the University and taking three other players with him. Mrs. Biff Johnson had managed to get through Home Ec II, so Hortense was indeed going to see her daughter graduate. Patsy Kay said she was going to Memphis to beauty school—I could imagine how the future bridesmaids would look once *she* got a hold of them! I had a scholarship to the college I wanted to attend in the state capital. Sandy was already there and I knew she would show me around. I would continue to buck tradition and in years to come I would travel around the world. I would see Disneyland, Rome, China, and the even and the largest desert of them all, the Sahara. Hally was going to major in drama at the University—and she pledged KD, so the Pallet Party Queen would continue her social whirl. Claudia could not wait to get her car for not smoking. Sallybeth's mama had already gotten in all her Chi O recs to the University. A lot of people in town were thunderstruck when Teebo got an appointment to the Naval Academy at Annapolis—but I knew he would be God's gift to Naval Intelligence. I was greatly relieved that Teebo would now learn to swim. Travis Dexter Juvenile Delinquent had served his time at Bubba's, if indeed what we had heard had been true—and was going to the University to join the team with Trey. Jimmie Gayle had his own car to take to State. I did not know if Jimmie Gayle were taking the diary of Donald McQuaid with him.

I never asked what happened to it.